SIMPLIFIED DESIGN FOR BUILDING SOUND CONTROL

Other titles in the
PARKER–AMBROSE SERIES OF SIMPLIFIED DESIGN GUIDES

Harry Parker and James Ambrose
Simplified Design of Concrete Structures, 6th Edition

Harry Parker, John W. MacGuire and James Ambrose
Simplified Site Engineering, 2nd Edition

James Ambrose
Simplified Design of Building Foundations, 2nd Edition

James Ambrose and Dimitry Vergun
Simplified Building Design for Wind and Earthquake Forces, 3rd Edition

Harry Parker and James Ambrose
Simplified Design of Steel Structures, 6th Edition

James Ambrose
Simplified Design of Masonry Structures

James Ambrose and Peter D. Brandow
Simplified Site Design

Harry Parker and James Ambrose
Simplified Mechanics and Strength of Materials, 5th Edition

Marc Schiler
Simplified Design of Building Lighting

James Patterson
Simplified Design for Building Fire Safety

James Ambrose
Simplified Engineering for Architects and Builders, 8th Edition

James Ambrose
Simplified Design of Wood Structures, 5th Edition

William Bobenhausen
Simplified Design of HVAC Systems

SIMPLIFIED DESIGN FOR BUILDING SOUND CONTROL

JAMES AMBROSE

University of Southern California

JEFFREY E. OLLSWANG

University of Wisconsin-Milwaukee

A Wiley-Interscience Publication

JOHN WILEY & SONS, INC.

New York · Chichester · Brisbane · Toronto · Singapore

Library of Congress Cataloging-in-Publication Data:

Ambrose, James E.
    Simplified design for building sound control / James Ambrose,
Jeffrey E. Ollswang.
        p.   cm.
    Includes bibliographical references and index.
    ISBN 0-471-56908-9
    1. Soundproofing.   I. Ollswang, Jeffrey, 1946–   . II. Title.
TH1725.A57   1995
693'.834—dc20   94-23802

Printed in the United States of America

10 9 8 7 6 5 4 3 2 1

CONTENTS

PREFACE

This book is part of the Parker/Ambrose Simplified Design Series. It completes a set of three books, the other two treating the topics of lighting and HVAC (heating, ventilating, and air conditioning). These are the three main topics in general environmental control that most affect the form, materials, and details of buildings, and are consequently of major concern to building designers.

The topic of this book is the design for control of noise, privacy, and room acoustics in buildings. With the ever-increasing use of lighter construction materials and the steady increase of use of equipment that generates sound, this is a problem that continues and gets worse. This is not a book for acoustic engineers but for building designers who must consider sound problems and how they affect their design work.

The concentration here is on issues that relate to the decision-making process of the general building designer in the design process that flows from analysis of design criteria to the final choices for materials, products, and construction details. This book may serve as a text for a course on acoustic design for architects or as a self-study reference for persons interested in the general topic on a practical level.

Reading a book about sound is not unlike watching a silent movie about music. There are drastic limitations in how descriptions of sound effects can be achieved without hearing the sounds. Since our purpose here is not to *create* sounds but to get at how to construct buildings to respond to them, what we need most in the end is to deal with the *buildings,* not the *sounds.* In any event, with only text and graphics to work with, we must settle for trying to use the reader's experiences with sounds to evoke the sound conditions we describe.

We are grateful to the various people and organizations who have granted permissions for use of data and illustrations for this book. Acknowledgment of those sources is made where the materials are displayed in the book.

Sound problems in ordinary buildings (not theaters, sound studios, etc.) have traditionally been given little attention in the design stages. Dealing with them has mostly been a matter of postoccupancy remedial work. Our aim with this work is to encourage designers to get the design horse before the constructed building cart. It is really not that big a problem, and a great deal more efficient, as well as being much better for client relations.

JAMES AMBROSE
JEFFREY OLLSWANG

March 1995

SIMPLIFIED DESIGN FOR BUILDING SOUND CONTROL

INTRODUCTION

The purpose of this book is to provide a source of study and reference for the topic of sound as it pertains to the design of buildings. The treatment of the subject here is aimed at persons not trained in acoustics or the science of sound in general, but who desire some knowledge of the topic as it relates to building design and construction.

Some material relating to the general scientific fields of sound and human hearing is presented to provide a minimum background for the understanding of a few basic principles. However, the presentation and bulk of the materials focus on practical issues affecting design judgments and choices for construction materials and methods.

There are many excellent references available for those who wish to pursue this topic in any of its many special concerns. Some basic reference sources are listed in the Bibliography.

It is generally assumed that readers of this book have limited preparation in mathematics, and that, in general, they have little interest in extensive mathematical computations. Although mathematics must be used for an understanding of some basic principles, there is little need for highly deliberate mathematical derivations in order to understand the simple relationships and variables relating to fundamental phenomena.

Computations for simple cases can serve to demonstrate the effects of variables and the general procedures for investigation and design. For these purposes some example computations are shown here. This can help to give some appreciation for data used for design.

It is assumed that readers have some familiarity with basic issues in building planning, general development of building construction, and basic requirements of building codes. Lack of this background will not preclude the ability to understand principles of sound but will limit the reader's appreciation of the relevance of some materials to basic issues in building design and construction.

Symbols

The following "shorthand" symbols are frequently used in the text and illustrations:

Symbol	Reading
>	is greater than
<	is less than
$\leqslant$	greater than or equal to
$\geqslant$	less than or equal to
6'	six feet
6"	six inches
Σ	the sum of
ΔL	change in L

Notation

To keep some form of consistency in this book, we use the following notation. Most of this is in general agreement with that used in building technology and acoustic engineering. The list here is limited to notation used in this book. Definitions of terms may be found in the Glossary or by use of the Index.

a	absorption coefficient in square feet (sabins)
A	gross (total) area of a surface or of a cross section
dB	decibel
Hz	cycles per second (hertz)
Rt	reverberation time in seconds
t	(1) thickness; (2) time

Greek letters:

Δ (delta)	change of
θ (theta)	angle
Σ (sigma)	sum of

1

BASIC CONCERNS

Architects ought to consider all aspects of buildings. However, as designers, they tend to deal first with those factors that have the greatest effects on choices of building form, construction materials and details, and the materials and textures of building surface finishes.

Obviously, development of the building construction and design of the structure are major concerns in this regard. In these times, however, building occupants tend to expect a high degree of comfort and a general lack of stress in their surroundings. The latter translates into high expectations of the building responses to the effects of heat, atmospheric conditions (air quality in general), light, and sound.

This book is the third volume in a three-book set that develops these primary environmental concerns. The focus here is on sound and the sound-related experiences of building occupants. This introductory chapter presents a general view of the common problems related to sound that may be of concern in building design.

1.1 SOUND PROBLEMS IN BUILDINGS

Sounds are all around us, and not all are "problems" for building designers or occupants. However, in modern times, especially in highly populated areas, we are indeed surrounded by and often disturbed by

Sound moves outwards - spherically - from the source.

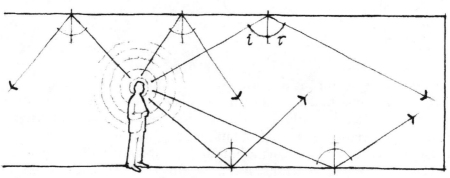

Geometric Acoustics assumes that:
   a. sound moves outwards - radially - in straight lines.
   b. the angle of incidence, i = the angle of reflection, r.

FIGURE 1.1   Sound emanates from various sources, moving mostly through the air in a spherically expanding form until interrupted. Inside enclosed spaces, it is typically interrupted considerably by the bounding surfaces and other objects in the space. The net effect for listeners in buildings is a modified condition for hearing that is often strongly influenced by elements of the building construction. This gives the building designers much to deal with in the manipulation or control of sound affects.

unwanted and unpleasant sounds. Decisions by building designers cannot deal fully with the problems of sound, but to the extent that they can affect some control of sound, it becomes another source of criteria for informed design. (See Fig. 1.2 and 1.3.)

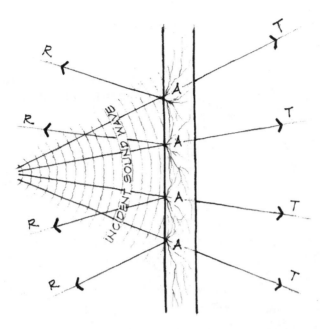

FIGURE 1.2 Effect of an obstacle in the sound path. Of the total sound energy received, part is absorbed (A), part is reflected back (R), and part is transmitted (T) through or around the object.

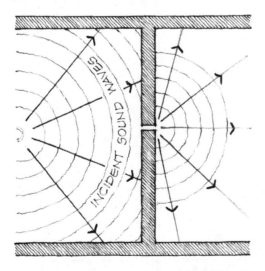

FIGURE 1.3 In various ways, the sound that passes through or around a barrier is modified. Thus the opposite side of a partition wall becomes a new sound source, emanating a modified version of the sound received by the other side of the wall.

There are three main areas of concern for design for sound management:

Room Acoustics. This is the general experience of sounds *within* an enclosed space (room); often related to particular sounds in spaces having specific uses. (See Fig. 1.4.)

Sound Privacy. This has generally to do with sound transmission from space to space by various paths, including through the building construction. Privacy has a double meaning; it includes security of one's private conversations and the occupying of a space essentially free of uncontrolled, intruding sounds.

Noise Control. Noise is generally defined as unwanted sound. It may come from just about any source, even beautiful music or friendly voices if you are trying to sleep. When the term *noise control* is used with regard to building design, however, it frequently refers to sounds generated within the building by equipment, plumbing, ducts, and so on. Control may deal with both suppression at the source and reduction in transmission. (See Fig. 1.5.)

Noise control and sound privacy are most often accomplished by some combination of *sound insulation* or *sound isolation.* Insulation is typically achieved by absorption of the transmitted sound, while isolation is achieved by some form of interruption of the sound transmission or by other means of separation of the listener from the sound source.

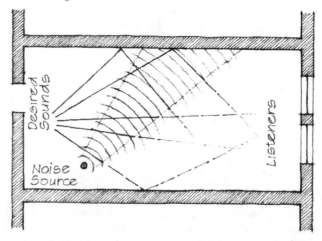

FIGURE 1.4 Room acoustics. Inside a room, listeners receive sound from a source as a combination of direct and reflected sounds waves. Also affecting the specific listening task is the general, enduring sound level in the room, called the ambient background noise level.

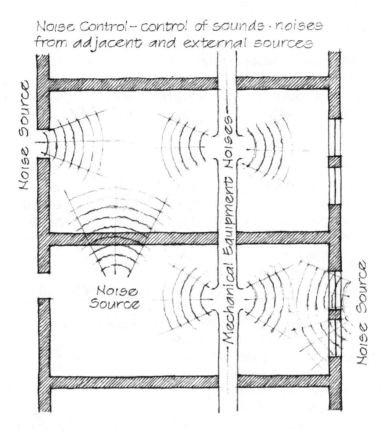

FIGURE 1.5   In the general case for noise control, listeners must deal with noises that enter through openings in the room enclosure, are transmitted from adjacent spaces through common barriers, and are transmitted through the continuous construction from remote locations in the building.

Sound control problems for the building designer may develop in any of these areas, having to do with a variety of common circumstances. Often, efforts made to improve conditions for one situation may improve conditions for other situations as well. However, the three areas of concern previously described also have very specific considerations.

Typical problems defined in terms of the experience of building occupants are the following:

Noisy rooms in which it is difficult to listen and communicate. The noise may be incoming (noise control and privacy problems) or may basically be a matter of room acoustics (hard surfaces, enduring sound, etc.).

Adjacent spaces with sounds from one disturbing the others. This is a common situation in apartments, offices, schools, and many buildings with multiple interior spaces. Many things may affect the situation, and simple good planning to separate spaces may be the easiest solution.

Noise generated by necessary building equipment or services. This is transmitted (possibly along with sensible vibrations) to occupied spaces, disturbing concentration on work or simply creating unpleasant conditions. Typical culprits: toilets, air-conditioning units, large fans, gurgling pipes, whistling ducts, slamming doors. This requires a coordinated design effort, beginning with design consideration of the offending items themselves by specialists in plumbing and mechanical equipment.

Intrusion of exterior sounds into buildings through the construction envelope. This is a general problem in highly populated urban areas with considerable traffic, or any buildings near major sound sources such as airports. This must generally be solved with careful attention to the materials and construction details for the roof and exterior walls, including doors and windows.

Most of these problems can and should be anticipated and dealt with in early stages of design. Effective means for control may simply be a matter of correct choices in building planning or the selection of construction materials. However, there may be some unavoidable costs involved in achieving special properties of the construction; notably substantial reduction of sound transmissions through the construction itself where the preferred materials have little inherent resistance.

Sound is made into a problem by the people who use buildings and the tolerance or sensitivity they have for sound. While technical measurement of sound properties of inanimate objects (the building's parts) may be achieved precisely, sound experiences of people are considerably subjective. Quantified design criteria for sound design based on human responses are derived primarily from long experience of acceptable or tolerable situations.

1.2 NOISE

The general term *noise* covers a wide range of sounds and conditions. Noise is a problem when it intrudes and interferes with a listening or communication task. Except in hermetically sealed containers, some noise is always present, and it becomes a problem only when it intrudes and becomes a competing source or actually drowns out other sounds.

Noise may also be qualified as such by the attitude or conditioning of the listener. City folks may sleep blissfully through the enduring nighttime urban traffic noise, while country visitors are highly disturbed. This makes for a lot of very soft targets for the designer and a very sketchy possibility for fully achieving the satisfaction of clients. Clients should be educated to this problem.

There are basically three ways for the designer to consider dealing with noise problems; and all three may be pursued in some situations.

1. Suppress the noise source. Specify equipment with low ratings for noise output; use shock-absorbing mountings; encase equipment in sound-insulating enclosures.
2. Reduce noise levels during transmission. Place the source as far as possible from the listeners; make it lose its energy in passing through the construction.
3. Isolate the listener from the noise. Create a constructed enclosure (walls, floors, ceilings) that filters or impedes the transmission of the noise into the space occupied by the listener.

A first step in handling noise is to make a careful analysis at early design stages of both the potential noise sources and the sensitive listening and communication tasks in a building. The rankest amateur designer would hopefully not place the boss's office next to the employees' rest rooms, or the rooftop air conditioner directly over a conference room.

1.3 SOUND PRIVACY

Many trends of our times make the achieving of privacy an increasingly difficult challenge for building designers. Some of these factors are noted below.

Clients hold higher expectations. Today's building owners and occupants are generally more attuned to their "rights" in terms of the accountability of those providing their constructed environments. They expect and demand better performance.

Steadily increasing noise levels. We all own more equipment and appliances (hair dryers, high-fidelity stereo systems, TV sets, air conditioners, clothes dryers, food processors, power tools, etc.) and use them more (115 channels on cable TV). We generate more traffic noise on the ground and in the air.

Closer packing of people. Space becomes more precious, more expensive, less available. Most of the population lives in multiple housing; single-family houses are on tighter sites and only a few feet apart.

More sound transparent building construction. We want light! So we have more windows, skylights, balconies, and patios. Exterior walls, roofs, partitions, and floors are made ever flimsier and more flexible. Increasing services cause more penetrations.

Put it all together and the situation for happy sound environments becomes an ever more frantic quest—and a more serious issue for designers.

Architects, of course, are not the only ones being pressured by this situation. Builders, product manufacturers, and building owners are also under the gun. As a result, there is a steady growth in the inventory of sound-qualified building products and sound-tested building techniques. The real task for the building designer—after achieving some reasonable awareness of the issues—is to get on top of the current technology.

1.4 AUDIBILITY

A particularly difficult sound problem is that of audibility, which is basically a subjective—although very real—phenomenon for individual listeners. Can you hear what you want to hear? This will be a matter of comfort or ideal listening conditions. It may also be very critical to specific and difficult listening tasks.

Once defined, specific listening tasks may be analyzed reasonably accurately in technical terms. These may deal both with the sound itself and its various properties and with the physiology and psychology of "hearing" by the listener. Effects of the hearing environment (room acoustics, privacy, intruding noises) may be incorporated in the analysis. Finally, a prediction or diagnosis may be made for the qualified nature of the listening task.

This kind of investigation provides for what we can use in some quantified design response to the accommodating of listening tasks. In the end, however, the judge is the person trying to execute the listening task. A principal problem is the range of capabilities of the members of the human race: young and old, hearing healthy and hearing impaired, relaxed or disoriented, concentrated or distracted.

For design purposes, creating good listening situations must usually be bracketted to concentrate on a range that is most predictable as adequate for most listeners. This may produce sound conditions that are somewhat boring for persons with good hearing, but is a way to maximize audibility for large groups.

1.5 SPECIAL PROBLEMS

The basic, most common issues were presented briefly in the preceding sections of this chapter. Following common building design and construction practices often means making some default provisions for these, even when designers do not make much conscious effort to "design" for sound.

Sound emerges as a *problem* most often when some very special sound situation is encountered. Some examples of these are discussed next.

Room Acoustics

Every room in a building deserves some attention for its internal sound environment. However, the full bag of tricks for room acoustics is usually reserved for those special spaces where sound is a major aspect of the room use. Theaters, concert halls, lecture rooms, sound stages, and recording studios are such places, and the highest art of acoustic specialists should be applied to the design of these spaces.

This is an intensely developed subject, not yielding much to a "simplified" approach. We address some of the basic aspects of it and deal with some simple considerations for modest environments but cannot give a complete presentation of the state of the art in room acoustics for highly critical spaces.

Although the conditioning of the room itself is at the heart of dealing with room acoustics, it goes without saying that sound privacy and noise control must also be achieved before fine tuning of the room is approached. Thus dealing with the highest levels of room acoustics means handling the entire spectrum of potential sound problems in building design.

Enduring Sounds

This includes a number of phenomena that have to do with complex sound experiences; for example, *echoes.* For design purposes, we often consider a single sound and its singular behavior by wave theory and the physiology of hearing in response to it. However, real sound experience means an enduring condition of mixed sounds, including repetitions of the original single sound as it bounces around us.

A single note from a violin is already a complex sound as it originates from the instrument, but it becomes an enlarged experience within the enclosure of a concert hall as the room modifies the sound. The modification may glorify the original sound or distort it unpleasantly. And the distinction between the two effects may be thinly separated by very subtle changes in what is essentially a single physical behavior. The echo is born by a crossing of one of these thin lines, a potentially reinforcing reflected sound coming a little too late.

Focusing

Surrounding constructions (walls, ceilings, floors, large objects in a space) modify sound conditions by the sounds that bounce off them. A particular problem that often occurs is the concentration of this sound modification when there is some focal point where the bounced sounds may gather and magnify the sound unpleasantly. A common case is that occurring beneath a domed ceiling.

Focusing may be used constructively if managed carefully in lecture or concert halls. However, it becomes distracting or annoying more often at selected locations in large spaces with multiple listeners. It is also only one of a set of related phenomena, and situations with this potential will also usually need other investigations for problems.

Vibrations

Essentially, sound is transmitted by vibrations through the solid building materials and the air. These vibrations may become annoying or even painful and injurious in some situations, extreme loudness being an example. The vibrations can also be sensed by means other than hearing and may be disturbing from that viewpoint.

Sound transmission can be reduced by general reduction of the associated vibrations. Other vibrations—from building equipment, truck or rail traffic, slamming doors, and so on—may also be intercepted or moderated in the transmission. Thus building design for noise reduction is often associated with general design for reduction of vibrations. Vibration is vibration, and it may annoy us as a hearing problem, as a sensible motion problem, or as both.

1.6 SUMMARY: DESIGN GOALS AND CRITERIA

To do any design for sound it is necessary to establish design goals. These derive basically from some definable listening experience, what is sometimes called a *listening task*. Once such tasks are established, and the place where they occur in the building identified, it becomes a matter of some analysis of the sounds and the behavior of the listener in the situation.

Much experience over time with common situations, ordinary forms of construction, typical building planning, and various of *Murphy's laws*, has produced some guidelines for what may be expected to work and what can be expected to produce problems. Having some grasp of this cumulative knowledge the building designer may establish some meaningful, pragmatically achievable goals.

What can be done by architects and builders with only a minor education in acoustics may reasonably suffice for many ordinary situations. That is basically what this book is all about, and the various aspects of the problem are treated in the following chapters.

2

NATURE OF SOUND

A first task in learning to understand the effects of sound is to gain some familiarity with the basic laws of physics that govern the nature of sound, its behavior, and its effects on objects in general. In this chapter we present a digest of fundamental concepts and principles relating to the physics of sound. The descriptions will to a large extent employ the technique of *geometric acoustical analysis*, or more simply *geometric acoustics*, which consists of a graphic representation of sound propagation that allows for the visualization of what is most likely to happen as sound travels outward from its point of origin.

2.1 PHYSICAL CHARACTERISTICS

When a sound source (such as a violin string) vibrates in air, it creates a series of high and low *air pressure waves* that move away from the source. The sound waves reach the human ear, causing the eardrum to vibrate and producing the sensation of hearing. These vibrations are so minute they may not be visible (except perhaps in the case of a plucked guitar string), but when conducted through solid materials, they can often be felt. They do have very definite physical characteristics, which can be measured with the aid of electronic instruments.

The generated sound waves travel through the air in the form of small pressure changes, alternately above and below a static atmospheric pressure: the ever-present air pressure that is measured by a barometer. The average deviation in pressure above or below static value, called *sound pressure*, is related to the loudness of a sound.

A sound wave is one complete cycle or vibration, from normal pressure, through high pressure, back to normal, through low pressure, and back to normal pressure again, completing one entire sound-wave cycle. These high–low pressure combinations are propagated parallel to the motion of the wave and thus produce *longitudinal* waves.

The number of times this cycle occurs in 1 second is the *frequency* of the wave. For example, if a train whistle has a frequency of 344 cycles per second, then 344 separate high–low pressure combinations will strike the eardrum each second. The unit of measure of frequency is termed *hertz*, representing 1 cycle per second and abbreviated *Hz*.

Every sound, musical or otherwise, has a specific frequency—the number of complete vibrations that occur in 1 second. The frequency of the source is constant because it is a function of the mass or density and the elasticity of the vibrating source object. Whether a piano key is struck lightly or forcefully, the string will vibrate at the *same* frequency; only the pressure or amplitude of the sound will be different. The interrelationships are illustrated in Figure 2.1.

The rate at which the sound waves progress through a conductor is called *velocity*, or more commonly, *speed.* It plays a significant role in architectural acoustics because it is relatively slow (compared to the speed of light, for example). This factor becomes important when we deal with the control of sound reflections.

While sound commonly travels directly by air alone, it travels much faster and with less loss of energy when conducted through solid materials. For example, an impact noise against the steel frame of a building can quickly telegraph the vibration throughout a large structure with very little loss in pressure. It will be heard distinctly throughout the building because sound waves will be created in the air in response to the vibrating structure.

The composition of the conductor affects travel speed. Sound waves travel in air at a uniform rate of about 1128 feet per second at 70°F. In a solid conductor such as steel, the rate is 18,000 feet per second. In wood, the rate is about 12,000 feet per second.

Sound speed is greater in solid materials because of density and elasticity—the stronger intermolecular forces rebound (after compression) much more quickly than in air. Velocity varies only with the physical nature of the conductor; it does not change with the frequency or amplitude of the sound.

The *wavelength* of a sound is the distance between the same point in two consecutive waves (Figure 2.1). The frequency of the sound and the speed of travel determine the wavelength. Since the speed of sound in any particular conductor is constant, frequency becomes the principal variable. As the frequency of sound vibrations is increased, wavelength decreases because the vibrations are leaving the source at a uniform rate (see Fig. 2.3). Wavelengths traveling in the air vary in size from as little as $\frac{11}{16}$ inch for 20,000-Hz sounds to $56\frac{1}{2}$ feet for 20-Hz sounds. These two waves represent

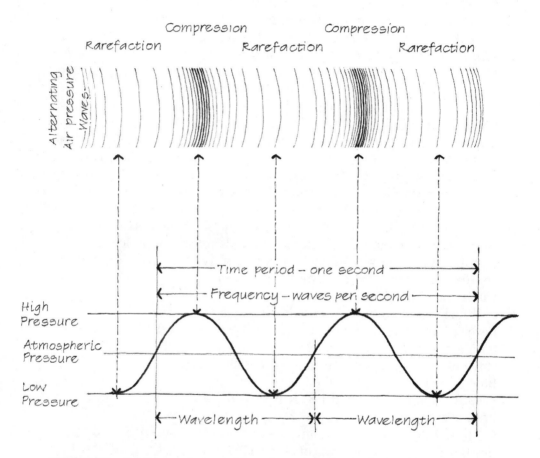

FIGURE 2.1   Basic form of a sound wave for a pure tone (enduring, constant, single-frequency sound). Vertical plot is pressure variable from a neutral position represented by the unmodified condition of the transmitting medium (atmospheric pressure for air). The horizontal plot is time. The amplitude of the vibration (maximum distance of displacement from the neutral condition) indicates the sound pressure or apparent loudness of the sound. The time for one complete wave represents the frequency (actually the period; the frequency is the inverse of the period). Frequency can also be defined as the number of complete waves occuring in a unit of time (1 second). The wavelength is determined by the combined properties of the period for one full wave and the velocity of travel of the pressure waves in the transmitting medium.

the usual maximum and minimum frequencies that can be heard by human beings with very good hearing capability.

The amplitude of the wave represents the *intensity* of the energy level produced by the vibrating source. It is measured in sound pressure units and is represented by the displacement of the pressure layers as the wave travels through a conductor. It is diagrammed as the vertical dimension above or below the static atmospheric pressure line in Figure 2.1. It corresponds to the loudness of the sound.

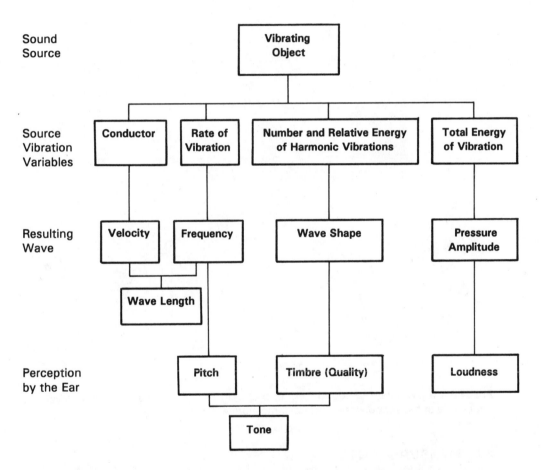

FIGURE 2.2 Sound propagation from a source to a listener. The originating source establishes various physical properties of the sound vibration and its development as variable sound pressure in a transmitting medium (air, water, solid). The propagation from the source is in wave form, with various fundamental properties of the waves. Reception by a listener results in various factors of perception, the major ones being loudness, pitch, and quality.

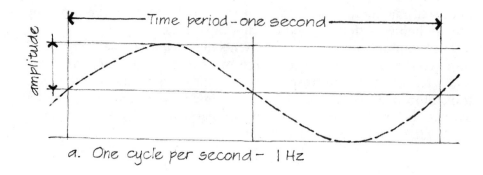

a. One cycle per second – 1 Hz

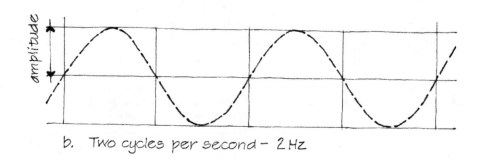

b. Two cycles per second – 2 Hz

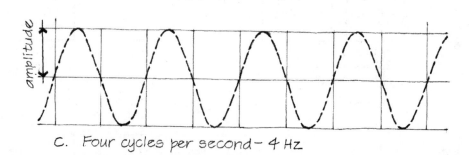

c. Four cycles per second – 4 Hz

FIGURE 2.3 Variation of sound frequency (pitch) at constant sound energy level (amplitude of the sound wave, general indication of loudness).

2.2 MEASUREMENTS

In physics sound pressure is measured as force per unit area, the common units being watts/cm². For our purposes a more useful measurement is a relative one that compares pressures to a reference loudness as perceived by the human ear. This relates directly to human response, which is our primary concern for building design.

To measure the relative pressure of different sounds, the *decibel* is used (abbreviated *dB*). It is equal to 20 times the logarithm of the ratio of sound pressure to a reference pressure of 0.0001 watts/cm^2:

$$\text{sound pressure level (dB)} = 20 \log_{10} \frac{\text{measured pressure}}{\text{reference pressure}}$$

This is a convenient tool to indicate the *ratio* of loud sounds to softer ones. For example, a sound with 10 times the pressure of another is considered to be 20 dB louder. Each succeeding 10-fold increase in pressure adds another 20 dB to the level of sound.

The decibel measure gives a rough connection between the physical intensity of sound and the subjective loudness it causes. It enables us to handle a tremendous range of sound pressures. In Table 2.1 we list data relating to the issue of loudness of sounds as perceived by human listeners.

In Table 2.1 commonly experienced sounds are identified in terms of their perceived loudness. Values are given for sound pressures measured directly in watts/cm^2 and in decibels. Notice in the table that the ear is sensitive through a range of pressures of 10 million to one. Also that the ear's response to increasing pressure drops off very quickly as the level increases.

A change in pressure of approximately 3 dB generally represents the smallest change in loudness that the average person can sense. For measuring ordinary sounds, a decibel level of zero at 1000 Hz represents the faintest sound audible to the average person. Conversation level for most people is about 50 to 70 dB. Sounds become physically painful (and damaging) above 130 dB.

When considering loudness in terms of decibels, it is necessary to remember that the decibel notation uses a logarithmic scale. Thus, the adding of two sounds is not arithmetic; that is, two 50 *dB* sounds do not add up to a 100 *dB* sound but rather to approximately 53 *dB*.

It should also be noted that, although a 3 *dB* sound difference may be barely perceived as a change in loudness, it is usually takes at least a difference of 6 to 10 *dB* to be significantly perceived. For an easy reference, it may be noted that an increase of 10 *dB* is generally perceived as a doubling of the loudness (60 *dB* is twice as loud as 50 *dB*).

Perceived loudness and general audibility of sounds for human listeners depend on the combination of sound pressure level and the frequency of the sound vibrations. This combined response is illustrated in the set of equal-loudness curves in Figure 2.5. The figure shows that in the middle frequencies (from about 500 to 6000 Hz), far less sound pressure is

TABLE 2.1 SOUND PRESSURE LEVEL AND APPARENT LOUDNESS

Apparent Loudness	Examples	Sound Pressure Level		
		Decibels (dB)	Ratio to 0 dB	Watts/cm²
Deafening, very uncomfortable	Jet airplane or thunder, nearby	130+	8,000,000+	10^{-3}
Very loud, disturbing, prevents listening tasks	Speeding train, nearby	120	1,000,000	10^{-4}
	Chainsaw, nearby	110	316,200	
	Noisy factory, inside	100	100,000	10^{-6}
	Very noisy office; busy urban street	90	31,620	
	Average noisy office; busy restaurant	80	10,000	10^{-8}
Loud, makes listening difficult	Average street noise	70	3162	
	Typical large office; busy store	60	1000	10^{-10}
Moderate	Average restaurant; 2 person conversation	50	316	
	School classroom (with teacher); private office	40	100	10^{-12}
Quiet, faintly heard	Quiet bedroom; country nights	30	32	
	Wind in the trees	20	10	10^{-14}
Barely heard	One's own normal breathing	10	3	
	Defined threshold of audibility	0	1	10^{-16}

required to make tones equally audible than in the low- or high-frequency ranges. Due to the variation in loudness at different frequencies (but with the same energy), it is necessary to select a reference tone for determining loudness levels. The 1000-cycle frequency has been chosen for this purpose; thus the loudness of a sound is defined as the pressure level (in decibels) of a 1000-cycle sound that is equally loud.

While the extreme ranges for listening are shown in Figure 2.5, a more practical consideration is for the usual ranges involved in the common

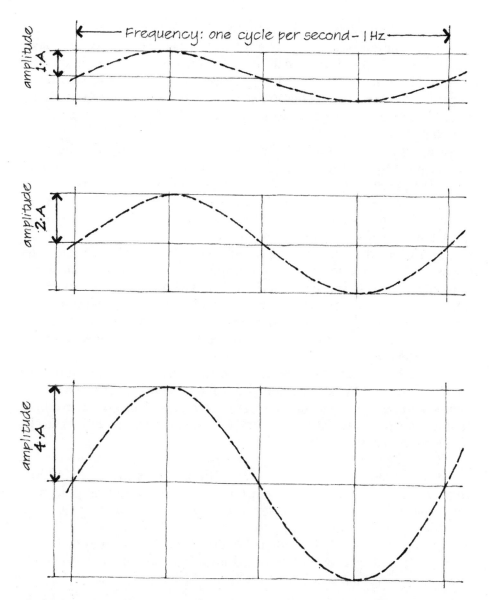

FIGURE 2.4   Variation of energy level (loudness) at constant frequency (pitch).

hearing tasks that human being's encounter. In Figure 2.6 the outer boundaries of the hearing range are represented by the top and bottom curves and the right and left edges of the graph. Within these limits, the common boundaries of orchestral music and human conversation are shown by the shaded loops. For practical design tasks, much of the concern will be for sounds that are within these boundaries.

2.3   SUBJECTIVE RESPONSE TO SOUND

When sound pressures reach the listener, the eardrums vibrate, producing the sensation of hearing. The intensity level of the sound pressure combined with its frequency determines a *judgment* of the loudness of the sound. The inner hearing mechanism, consisting of sensitive nerve endings, also enables the listener to determine *pitch* and *timbre* (also, direction by the inequality of loudness). Figure 2.2 illustrated the link of hearing to the sound source.

As discussed in Section 2.2, there is an important distinction between sound pressure and loudness. Pressure, resulting from the maximum high–low pressure variations of the wave, is a physical property that can be measured precisely but loudness is a subjective hearing response governed by the combination of frequency and intensity of the sound pressure level of sounds, as shown in Figure 2.6.

Fortunately, the loudness of a sound is not directly proportional to its pressure. A natural defense mechanism in the ear reduces its sensitivity automatically as the pressure increases. Thus the tremendous pressure of an explosion does not sound many thousands of times louder than a cat's meow, even though the sound pressure difference may be that great. The hearing organs are sensitive to sounds over an enormous range of sound pressure levels.

Also, the ear is not equally sensitive to all sound frequencies, and some it does not detect at all (see Figure 2.5). Hence even though two different sounds produce the *same* sound pressure, one sound may be judged to be louder than the other if its energy is concentrated in a frequency where the ear is more sensitive.

The ear detects the frequency of a sound as *pitch* (the term *tone* is often used synonymously with the word *pitch* although it also infers a combination of pitch and timbre in many instances). The frequency range from 20 to 20,000 Hz is audible to most people. Sounds with frequencies near 20,000 Hz are very high pitch and those at the other end of the scale are very low pitch. The musical pitch of middle C has a frequency of 261 Hz. Very few pure-pitch sounds are heard since most sounds consist of combinations of numerous frequencies.

It is important for building designers to note how sensitivity to sounds drops off rapidly at the extreme low and high frequencies. This indicates that efforts to modify sound conditions should concentrate on the narrow band of frequencies to which the ear is most sensitive. In a direct physical way, this relates specifically to dimensions of sound wavelengths and to the physical responses of building elements to specific frequencies.

2.4 STRUCTURE OF SOUNDS

Sound quality, or *timbre*, enables us to distinguish one voice or musical instrument from another even though the sound is not unique in pitch and loudness. It depends on the structure and pattern of sounds, which causes us to distinguish between *pure tones*, *overtones*, and *harmonics*, all of which are frequency dependent. The audible frequency range permits a practically unlimited number of sound combinations.

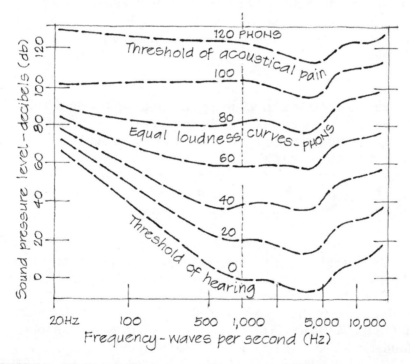

FIGURE 2.5 Equal loudness curves (phons). Perceived loudness is a combination of sound pressure level and frequency. The decibel scale is based on sound pressure at a frequency of 1000 Hz. Equivalent loudness occurs at other pressure levels at different frequency. The curves connect these points for selected decibel levels. This illustrates the concentration of sensitivity of the ear to particular frequencies and the narrow range of frequencies that affect audibility.

Harmonics

A recording of the sound wave of a single-frequency tone (Figure 2.2) produces a symmetrical graph of smoothly curving peaks and valleys, all equally spaced. Pure tones consisting of a single frequency without any overtones (such as those produced by a tuning fork) are highly unusual in architectural situations; they are most apt to be found only in testing laboratories.

A *harmonic* (or overtone) is a secondary tone of a frequency that is a whole-number *multiple* of the frequency of the dominant pitch (fundamental tone). In musical terms, the interval in one *octave* represents a doubling of the frequency. For example, a sound of 440 cycles per second is one octave above a sound of 220 cycles. The two sounds will have an audible relation to each other (for instance, the tuned relationship between middle C and the C note that is one octave higher).

Harmonics provide the full-bodied quality to musical tones that make them pleasing to the ear. The more harmonics that can be heard, the richer and fuller the sound. A recording of nonmusical noise would look like a multitude of short, sharp peaks that lack the periodic qualities of musical sound—again because of a lack of harmonics.

Complex Sounds

Sound waves from any source are usually made up of a number of different single-frequency (or simple-harmonic) waves. The relative intensity, loudness, and combinations of harmonics produce the quality of sound and enable the ear to identify specific sounds.

Figure 2.7 shows the combination of a fundamental tone with a harmonic. The resulting complex wave, displayed in graph form as an *oscillogram*, is actually the sum of the two simple waves, one with twice the frequency of the other.

Figure 2.7 also shows graphs of typical complex sound waves produced by sounds of the same pitch. The fundamentals of the tones are the same, but the quality is different in each case because of the variation in harmonics. Note that the waveform for these tones repeats at definite time intervals defined by the frequency. In short, the ear detects and identifies sounds by the way in which the higher-frequency overtones combine with the fundamental tone to produce the final waveform.

Wavelengths

The final structural aspect of sound that must be addressed is the physical size of sound waves, described as wavelength. Wavelength is related to frequency. To control sounds through reflection or surface absorption requires that an object be placed in the sound path that is equal to or larger than the size of the sound wavelength.

This is particularly important when dealing with lower frequency sounds that have large wavelengths. In geometric acoustics it is generally recognized that manipulations of reflections are effective for sounds down to only about 250 Hz and associated wavelengths smaller than 4 ft. Below that range the sounds with really large wavelengths will travel outward from the source just about any way they want to.

2.5 SOUND TRAVEL

Before we can control sound, we must understand its behavior under varying conditions and influences of its environment. Figure 2.8 indicates the direct path and the possible influences on an indirect path of sound to the human ear. These influences are produced by the shape, size, and

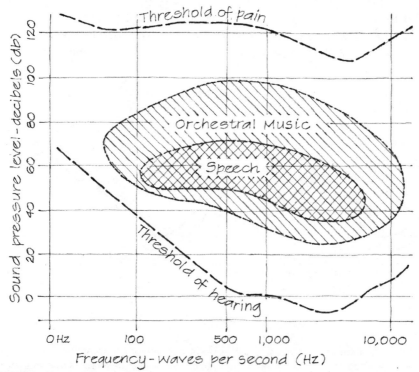

FIGURE 2.6 Positions of speech and wide-range (orchestral) music in the range of hearing capability of the human ear. The horizontal plot of the graph indicates the extreme ranges of 0 and 10,000 Hz sound frequency. The upper and lower loudness limit curves are the zero and 120-dB equal loudness curves shown in Figure 2.5. For speech audibility there may be observed to be a much smaller range. Critical sound and noise control concentrates on this smaller range of greatest influence.

physical nature of the obstacles and surfaces of the space in which the sound originates and is heard.

In a space free from reflecting surfaces, sound travels outwards spherically from the source in a *direct* sound path. Each listener will hear only the portion of the overall sound wave that is traveling in a direct line to the listener's ear. As the distance from the source increases, the sound pressure at the listener's ear will decrease by the inverse square law.

In an enclosed space with reflective surfaces, the listener will eventually hear nearly all of those portions of the sound wave traveling in other directions by virtue of the reflections from the surfaces (Figure 2.9). As the distance between the listener and the source increases, the importance of the *reflected sound* increases.

Sound reflections can be multiple and frequent in a room with few absorptive surface materials. The simplest form of sound reflection occurs when sound waves strike a *flat* surface, as shown in Figure 2.9. As the waves strike the surface, they rebound, creating new wave fronts directed at an angle equal to the angle at which they struck the surface.

The loudness of reflected sounds perceived by the listener will usually be less than that of a direct sound, because of the longer travel distance and also because of the energy loss at the reflecting surface due to *absorption* (see Figure 2.8). However, the combined effect of reflected and direct

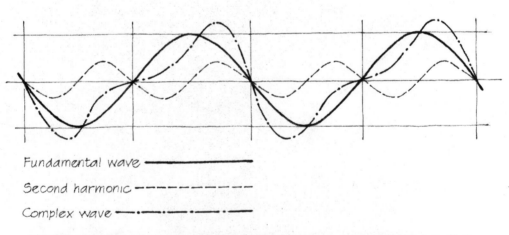

Fundamental wave ———————

Second harmonic — — — — — — —

Complex wave —·——·——·——·—

FIGURE 2.7 Complex sounds. Most sounds consist of combinations of multiple individual sounds occurring simultaneously to produce a single effect. A dominant tone or major, fundamental frequency may be present, but is accompanied by many other frequencies at various pressure levels that condition the sound. The stronger the dominant frequency, the more "pure" the tone; the less noticeable the dominant frequency, the more a "fuzzy" or broad-range sound is perceived (like having all the instruments in an orchestra playing at once). Test instruments may record a very complex sound, but the human ear will tend to pick up mostly the dominant frequencies, especially if they are concentrated in the range of highest sensitivity (500 to 5000 Hz).

sound will be louder than the direct sound alone. Reflected sound is often desirable in large enclosures to *reinforce* the direct sound and provide more uniform distribution over the entire audience area. Positive sound reinforcement may be accomplished by controlling reflections in terms of time and distance (see Figure 2.9). As the listener is further away from the sound source, these reflections become more important.

If the time interval between the direct and reflected sounds reaching the listener is less than 0.6 seconds, the reflections will probably reinforce

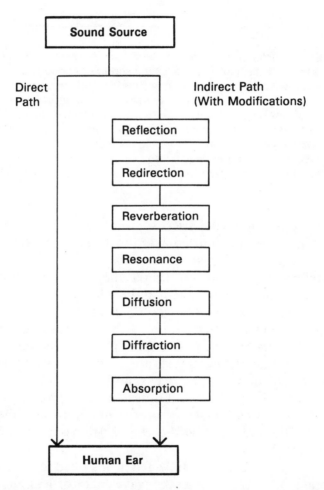

FIGURE 2.8 Sound travel and hearing. Airborne sound in an enclosure travels by both direct and reflected paths. The direct travel is affected mostly only by the distance between the source and the listener. Reflected paths may be conditioned by many potential modifications, allowing for a considerably different sound as received by a positioned listener in the space. The chief means for modification by architectural design have to do with adjustments of the reflected sounds. However, other factors can make significant contributions: notably structure-borne sounds, incoming noise, sustained background noise, or use of an amplified sound system.

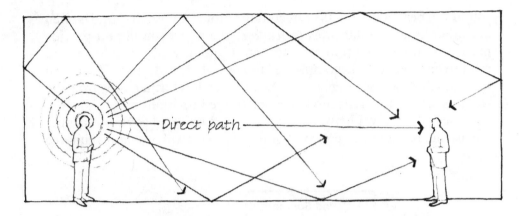

FIGURE 2.9 Geometry of sound travel. Sound waves travel in direct lines until deflected by various effects, mostly by reflecting surfaces. Although the sound may be directed from the source (direction the speaker is facing), it propagates essentially in a spherical manner from the source (in all directions). Thus virtually *every* surface that can be seen from the point of origin of the sound is a potential reflector. The reflected sounds may be beneficial to listeners (as reinforcement of the direct sound) or be distracting (as excess reverberation, echoes, etc.). Almost every reflector will modify the reflected sound to some degree, which also may be beneficial or reduce audibility or purity for the listener at any given location.

and not mask or muddle the direct sound. The smaller the time interval the better. This translates into a maximum distance difference of 65 ft between the direct and reflected sound paths.

When reflected sounds are not desired, the simplest methods for reducing their effects are to absorb them at the reflecting surfaces or to shape the reflecting surfaces to aim reflections away from listeners.

The perpetuation of reflected sound within a space after the source has ceased is called *reverberation*. The time interval between reflections is usually so short that distinct echoes are not heard. Instead, this series of reflections will blend with the direct sound to add "depth."

Reverberation time is defined as time required for sound to die down to one-thousandth of its original pressure (a 60-dB drop) after the source has stopped. After this time interval, the reverberation is no longer significant to the listener.

Sound waves are not always reflected or absorbed immediately. When an obstacle is the same size as the wavelength or less, the sound can "bend" around obstacles or flow through small openings and continue onward. This is called *diffraction*.

Sound will travel through a very small opening with surprisingly small loss of energy. A door closed to within an inch or two for a private conversation might as well be completely open for all the privacy it affords. Also, sound will pass through a perforated plate with virtually no loss if the opening represents at least 10% of the total plate area.

Upon contact, instead of reflecting, the wavefront breaks up, creating a new set of waves. The obstacle or the sound-leak opening sets up a secondary sound source, sending out waves of the same frequency and wavelength as the original but of lower amplitude.

Sound waves can reflect repeatedly between the walls, floor, and ceiling of a vacant room. But in a room with furniture, rugs, curtains, or acoustical tile, the waves enter these surfaces and bounce around aimlessly in the multitude of air pockets until they have lost much of their energy. When the sound finally escapes, most of its energy has been transformed into heat. The sound energy lost is said to be *absorbed* by the reflecting surface.

The amount of sound absorbed is measured in *sabins.* One sabin is equal to the sound absorption of 1 square foot of perfectly absorptive surface (theoretical, since no such surface exists).

Hard, massive, nonporous surfaces, such as plaster, masonry, glass, and concrete, absorb generally less than 5% of the energy of striking sound waves and reflect the rest. At the other extreme, acoustical products can absorb 90% or more of the energy.

Sound may react with its surroundings very strikingly in the form of *resonance.* This is the reinforcement of a tone by waves of identical frequency from another sound source. Every object or material is characterized by its natural frequencies of vibration. When the object is struck by sound waves of the same frequency as its natural frequency, it vibrates freely, acting as a second sound source. It produces waves nearly equal in pressure to the source and usually of considerably longer duration.

The walls and other surfaces and objects in theaters, concert halls, and auditoriums may be set in vibration by certain musical tones having a frequency equal to or very near the natural frequency of affected elements. Such responses are acoustically objectionable and require structural or decorative modifications designed to reduce the effect. Partitions may also become acoustically transparent at their natural frequencies, presenting an extra challenge to the design of sound control systems.

In buildings, sound also travels through the solid elements of the building construction. Sound traveling through the air is called *airborne sound*, while that traveling through the construction is called *structure-borne sound.* When the structural conductor is highly elastic and continuous— for example, steel frames, metal ducts, and piping—the sound travels very efficiently to remote locations with little loss of energy, there becoming airborne and heard distinctly by listeners.

2.6   SUMMARY: APPLICATIONS TO DESIGN

The many physical properties of sound, variables that affect its transmission and propagation, and subjective responses of listeners all bear on the general experience with sounds in buildings. The more one understands the basic principles and issues of sound behavior, the more likely that conscious design efforts can be made to improve sound conditions in the designed and constructed building.

With regard to sound and its behavior, the designer should accept the need to evaluate conditions for the following applications to design work.

1. *Anticipation of Problems.* Understanding the potential for problems and the need for consideration in the early stages of design should be a motivation for setting some design goals before any real design decisions are made. For the given project, what are the possible problems that can be expected, and what strategies can be used to avoid them or deal with them?

2. *Use of Data in Design.* Acoustic properties should be included with others in evaluating materials, products, and systems for construction. Effectiveness for sound control should be evaluated along with cost, structural safety, energy efficiency, and other concerns. Performance goals should relate to aspirations of owners and occupants.

3. *Planning for Sound Control.* Basic shaping of plans, arrangement of interior spaces, and forms for individual rooms should be considered for sound effects as well as other concerns. This is the most effective way to avoid problems, by eliminating them or at least by reducing them to a minimum rather than having to derive a complicated and expensive technical solution.

Means for achieving these are discussed in Chapters 4 through 7 and illustrated for the building cases in Chapter 8.

3

SOUND AND HEARING

Hearing is a primary physiological experience and a perceptive sensation that assists our general recognition of our environment. The essential body part involved is the ear, which receives sound vibrations directly and transmits an interpretation to the brain. Both the reception and transmission are subject to basic laws of physics but are also influenced by various subjective and conditioned responses. We like certain sounds and are disturbed by others, recognize familiar ones and are puzzled by strange ones, and each have some individual range of ability to perceive particular sounds. Some general rules apply to any hearing task, but specific interpretations are difficult to clarify for a general group of listeners because of the variations in individual hearing abilities. In this chapter we present some of the fundamental considerations for hearing as they concern the shaping of our built environment.

3.1 MECHANISM OF HEARING

Our fundamental perception of individual sounds has to do with the combination of their pitch (frequency in hertz) and perceived loudness (intensity in decibels). (See Figures 2.5 and 2.6.) As individuals, we have limits of perception of these separately. That is, we have high and low hertz limits, high and low pitch sounds we cannot hear. Dog whistles may be felt in some manner but not as ordinarily heard sounds. Very low pitch sounds may be felt as throbbing sensations without a conscious effect on the ear. A *normal* listener has a predictable range of hearing with regard to pitch which generally diminishes with age and can be affected temporarily or permanently by illness or some blockage of the ear canal (by a hand over the ear, by ear wax, etc.).

Deafness is most often interpreted as the inability to hear sounds of a normal range of loudness. The threshold of hearing is usually defined in terms of a decibel level at a specific frequency (Section 2.2). Again, there is some norm, but we all have specific limits; which, as for pitch, can be diminished by age, physical impairment, or illness.

The combination of pitch and loudness is interpreted in Figure 2.5, which relates to the measurement of sound sensitivity. In most regards, audibility as well as comfort (lack of disturbing noise) relate to the combinations illustrated. A very low intensity, sound at a frequency of 4000 Hz, for example, can be heard easily, whereas a much louder sound at a frequency of 50 Hz can barely be distinguished as sound at all. Evaluations for potential audibility and for disturbing noises will be made on the basis of this spectrum of pitch + loudness measurements.

Sound experienced in occupied spaces is usually also greatly affected by many other factors. These are discussed at length in Chapter 4.

3.2   SOUND SENSITIVITY AND AUDITORY SPECTRUM

Hearing sensitivity and the reasonably predictable range for the auditory spectrum for the human ear provide for the establishment of numerical limits for sound effects. Efforts to modify or to control sounds generally must concentrate on the range of sounds that are most critical. Basically, if we cannot hear a sound, we will not be disturbed by it and cannot be expected to respond to it for some hearing task.

Control of unwanted noises is most effective when it is concentrated on the range of sounds most likely to be heard, or in some cases, on those that may be most intrusive on a particular hearing task. Thus if we are trying to listen to a lecture, other sounds in the same frequency range as that of the human voice will interfere with our ability to hear and understand the lecturer. Efforts to suppress sounds being transmitted into the space of the lecture room should concentrate on interception of the selected range of sounds likely to be most disturbing. Reinforcement within the room should be given to the range of sounds that essentially constitute the lecturer's voice.

As discussed elsewhere, sounds in buildings (as vibrations) are transmitted both by air and by the building structure. While hearing is a singular experience, the sound path also affects the potential for audibility. Thus one set of numeric goals is derived for control of airborne sounds and another for structure-borne sounds. These distinctions are developed fully in Chapters 6 and 7.

3.3 AUDITORY TASKS, COMFORT, AND ACUITY

What constitutes a good hearing situation depends on what the listener is trying to do. This is generally defined as the *hearing task* or *listening task* and is a fundamental basis for definition of design goals or for evaluations for good or bad situations.

Hearing tasks may be defined in terms of individual actions of the listener, such as sleeping, listening to conversation, listening to music, and so on. However, as with other architectural design goals, tasks are more practically defined in terms of spatial occupancies, such as auditoriums, concert halls, classroom, offices, stores, restaurants, and so on.

Whether defined specifically for the listener or generally for the occupancy, critical hearing tasks can be measured in terms of the various factors that fundamentally affect hearing. For design purposes, however, achieving goals means defining tasks for the built environment. This leads to a whole other set of measured responses in terms of the effects of the built environment on sounds. In the end, the measured responses used for design are quite abstract with respect to the human listener. It is important, however, to appreciate their effectiveness by having some understanding of what they are truly trying to affect: the human listener.

In the following chapters we develop the issues of sound control in the built environment. The measured responses used for design are explained in those chapters. Specific situations and the practical means for realization of goals are treated more fully in the case studies in Chapter 8.

3.4 DISTRIBUTION OF SOUND: PATHS AND LISTENERS

In occupied spaces there are many possibilities for tasks and many types of sounds. For individual listeners it becomes important to place them in some location and to relate them to the experience at that location. For multiple listeners, if all are to have optimal hearing, it becomes necessary to have some reasonably uniform distribution of the sound.

Sound in rooms is distributed by a combination of direct and reflected paths. Individual listeners are located in some position with respect to the direct sound and the various reflections from different surfaces inside the room and possibly, with respect to any intrusive sounds that originate from outside the room.

Consideration of a hearing task starts with the nature of the original sound source (lecturer's voice, etc.). Hearing experiences relate to the direct sound path, to all the reflections as they are modified by time delays and the reflecting surfaces, and to the singular experience that becomes the combination of the multiple-sound sensations.

The sound paths—both direct and indirect—will relate to various physical properties of the sound (pitch, intensity, harmonics, etc.). Manipulation of the paths themselves may be possible by variations of the room planning—by positioning the sound origin and the listeners. Modifications of various kinds can also treat the various physical factors, such as room size, room shape, character of reflecting surfaces, obstacles in the sound path, and so on.

All of this obviously becomes more complicated when multiple tasks must be accommodated within a single space. This may involve origination of many different sounds: speaking in conversations, music, lectures, loudspeakers, or sound signals (alarms, etc.). Or it may involve a range of listeners: young and old, normal and impaired, single listener or groups.

Sound paths are also critical for control of intrusive sounds, that is, incoming noises. Control of these begins by distinguishing between airborne and structure-borne noises. Once inside the room, incoming noises are generally subject to the same modifications as those of sounds originating in the room. Their reduction, however, deals mostly with the control of their paths and modifications possible to achieve intensity reductions along the paths.

3.5 SUMMARY: DESIGN GOALS

The reason for developing design goals for acoustic performance is to ensure a comfortable and efficient environment for the human listener. If specific tasks or situations can be defined for the listener, they may serve as a basis for defined goals, either stated generally or prescribed specifically with measured performance criteria.

Establishing realistic and meaningful goals is complicated by the fact that there is really no such thing as a "normal" listener, even though such a state is necessarily defined by acoustic and hearing specialists. Being "normal" only means that you fit some statistical average; if you have more ability, you will perform listening tasks better but will be somewhat more disturbed by noises; if you have less ability, you will have to strain some for hearing tasks but will be happily insulated somewhat more from noises.

Defining the "norm" and using it for a design goal means that you will probably leave most listeners less than happy. Noise will disturb some more than others; hearing tasks will be easy for some and hard for others. Satisfying a range of listeners is a tough target.

Nevertheless, if you are going to make *any* quantified design computations or evaluations, you have to use some numbers, the numbers have to be based on some realistic reference limits, and the limits require a defined, "normal" listener. Just be sure that you understand the real significance and limitations of the numbers.

Because of its wide use for other building design classifications, the particular *occupancy* for a building or an individual room is most often used in defining performance goals. For buildings this means using office, school, store, assembly, housing, and other broad occupancy definitions.

For individual rooms there may be more specific task implications; thus in a house there will be rooms such as kitchen, bedroom, living room, recreation (family, rumpus) room, and so on. Various needs for performing specific hearing tasks may be defined for each type of space. Also of interest is the need for control of the construction barriers that separate spaces, such as when a bedroom is directly above the recreation (TV, game, party) room.

In the following chapters data from various sources are given for use in establishing design goals and limits. Performance to satisfy these goals is then the source of other criteria given for comparison with the rated properties of individual products or construction assemblages. This all gets very serious once the number crunching starts, but one needs to keep some perspective with respect to the issue mentioned previously regarding the significance of the "normal" listener.

4

ROOM ACOUSTICS

Room acoustics deals with the control and manipulation of sounds that are generated within a space. In this chapter we treat the basic concerns and general means for control of sound in enclosed spaces (rooms).

4.1 PROPAGATION AND DISTRIBUTION OF SOUND

The principal relationships and factors for sound propagation and distribution as they affect listeners were treated in the preceding chapters. As shown in Figure 2.9, individual listeners receive sound in some combination of direct and reflected sound waves. This is not a singular event but one that continues over time. Thus an additional problem is one of enduring sounds that affect other sounds in a continuous stream of hearing.

A single sound will produce an enduring effect primarily from the reflections that arrive after the direct sound waves. The net result may be one of reinforcement or may produce various disturbing effects, such as echoes or the blurring of other sounds. Evaluation of these conditions and any plans for modification for improvement of hearing must deal with all the significant factors that relate to the sound effects in the room and the hearing task of the listener.

4.2 SOUND PATHS AND REINFORCEMENT

To establish good room acoustics, one should reduce undesirable background noises while preserving and reinforcing desired sounds. This can be achieved effectively by the emphasis of useful sound reflections and the suppression of unwanted sounds.

In any space, the listener will first hear direct sound and then a series of reflections of that sound. In fact, most of the sounds heard in a space are the result of sound reflections rather than of direct sound (Figure 4.1). Therefore, a principal function of the enclosing surfaces of any space is to control sound reflections. First, reflective surfaces should be chosen and placed for the purpose of directing and distributing sound throughout the room. Second, absorptive surfaces should be designed and placed to prevent the continued presence of reflected sounds that are no longer useful reinforcement.

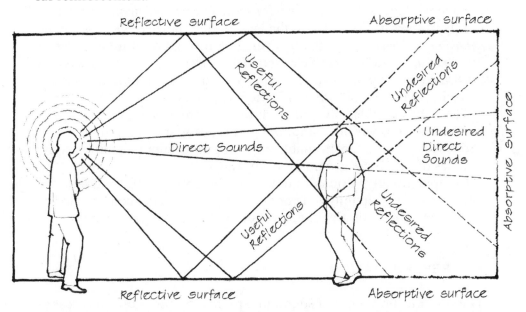

FIGURE 4.1 Effects of reflected sound. The combination of direct and reflected sounds can produce a singular listening experience that is perceived as fuller, richer, and deeper, and is possibly reinforced for full experience of rich music or heightened audibility of human speech. However, some reflections may tend to be distracting or actually interfere with good listening. Particularly distracting is the loss of orientation as to the direction of the source, which may occur if reflections from the side or rear are too strong. Thus the most potentially useful reflections tend to be those coming to the listener in the same general direction as the direct sound. This may not quite be true, however, if dispersed amplified sounds (speakers around the room) are added to the experience. It also depends somewhat on how the reflecting surfaces modify the sound, on reverbation, and on background noise levels.

For evaluation as sound-absorbing surfaces, various constructed finish surfacing is rated in sabins (a), which is a coefficient of efficiency compared with a perfect (100%) absorptive surface. The unit for sabins is square feet; thus a sabin rating of 1 ($a = 1.0$) means that the surface is 100% sound absorptive. A rating of $\frac{1}{2}$ ($a = 0.5$) indicates that it is equivalent to only one-half of 1 square foot in effectiveness, and thus reflects only one-half of the received sound. A rating of zero indicates a totally reflective surface, with no sound absorbed. A rating of higher than 1 is possible, indicating that the surface treatment actually serves partly to eliminate or extend the boundary surface, in effect making the room larger for sound behavior.

Sound absorption typically varies over the range of sound frequencies. Evaluations must therefore be made for the particular frequencies of most concern or for some average over a limited spectrum of frequencies. Table 4.1 lists absorption coefficients in sabins for various interior surface treatments. Table values are given for some selected frequencies, relating mostly to speech. The value in the last column, labeled NRC, is a *noise reduction coefficient*, obtained by averaging the values at frequencies of 250, 500, 1000, and 2000 Hz. Selection of these frequencies relates to issues illustrated in Figures 2.5 and 2.6. Table 4.2 lists some additional data for surfacing materials, showing only the NRC values.

The data in Tables 4.1 and 4.2 provide a small sampling of values obtainable from various handbooks. Values for specific products and various installations are available from the product manufacturers, some samples of which are given in the Appendix.

Computations of various kinds use the absorption coefficients and the total absorptive capability of room surfaces. One such computation is that for reverberation time, which is discussed in the next section.

4.3   REVERBERATION

The continued presence of sound in a room after the source has ceased generating it is *reverberation*. Reverberation time (Rt) is defined as the time it takes for a given sound to diminish to a level at which it is no longer perceptible in the space (see Figure 4.2). There is a direct and important relationship, therefore, between reverberation and background noise levels.

This raises two questions: When does a desirable sound reflection become an undesirable noise, and where and when should sound reflections be absorbed and terminated? The answers to both questions are simple. After the listener has heard the direct and reflected sounds, it is no longer helpful or advisable to have them persist in the room. At that point, sound reflections should be absorbed. Otherwise, their continued presence may interfere with the perception of the next desired sound.

TABLE 4.1 COEFFICIENTS OF ABSORPTION

Surface Development	Absorption Coefficients						
	125 Hz	250 Hz	500 Hz	1000 Hz	2000 Hz	4000 Hz	NRC
Gypsum drywall, $\frac{1}{2}$ in., single layer, on wood studs	0.10	0.08	0.05	0.03	0.03	0.03	0.05
Carpet with pad, on concrete fill or slab	0.02	0.06	0.14	0.37	0.60	0.65	0.29
Wood plank deck, cedar, etc.	0.24	0.19	0.14	0.08	0.13	0.10	0.14
Glass, ordinary window, small pane	0.35	0.25	0.18	0.12	0.07	0.04	0.15

TABLE 4.2   COEFFICIENTS OF ABSORPTION: NRC VALUES

Surface Development	NRC
Gypsum drywall, $\frac{1}{2}$ in., single layer, on wood studs	0.05
Wood or plywood panelling, $\frac{3}{4}$ in. thick	0.15
Plaster, hard finish, on concrete	0.05
Plaster, hard finish, on lath	0.05
Polished stone or ceramic tile	0
Concrete floor	0
Wood flooring	0.10
Thin floor tile, linoleum, etc.	0.05
Carpet with pad, on concrete fill or slab	0.29
Wood plank deck, cedar, etc.	0.14
Glass, ordinary window, small pane	0.15
Glass, large panes, thick plate	0.05
Mineral fiber ceiling tiles, average	0.50–0.75

For any room, for specific listening purposes, there is a desirable range for reverberation time: or, more subjectively, for a feeling of what is called either a "live" or "dead" sound condition. Excessively live rooms seem to ring with sounds that endure too long. Excessively dead ones give a feeling of being outdoors, unfettered by reflecting surfaces.

Many factors may contribute to a determination of reverberation time, but two primary ones are the total absorptive character of the room sur-

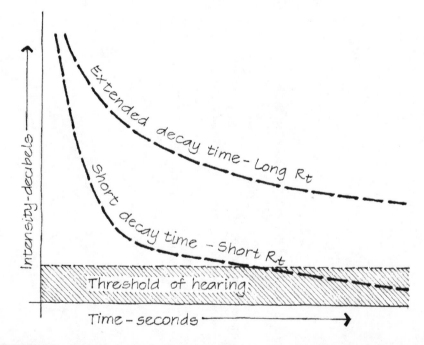

FIGURE 4.2   Enduring sounds. Reverberation is a measurement of sound endurance. Short reverbation time indicates rapid decay of the sound energy level. Long reverberation time indicates a long continuation or reinforcement of the original sound (extended decay time).

faces and the total volume of the room. This leads to a commonly used, simple formula for reverberation time as follows:

$$Rt = \frac{0.5V}{A}$$

where Rt = reverberation time in seconds

V = room volume in cubic feet

A = total absorption of room surfaces in sabins (in units of square feet)

In most design situations the room volume is a given constant, established by other design criteria. Thus the designer's most effective tool for manipulation of reverberation time is the modification of the absorption of the room surfaces.

Figure 4.3 shows the relationship between total sabins (absorption) and total volume for a room with respect to its apparent degree of liveness for sounds. Real accuracy is not possible here, as there are many additional variables, such as the proportion of room dimensions (length, width, height), the specific frequency of sounds, and the nature of the sound (for example, symphonic music versus a human voice speaking at conversation level).

Comparisons can also be made more directly between reverberation time and room volume, as shown in Figure 4.4. Since reverberation in general is highly critical for events such as musical concerts and lectures, the boundaries of the spectrum band of acceptability indicates what conditions favor these sound events.

Defining of optimal reverberation time is further blurred by the fact that the human ear cannot distinguish a decibel change of less than 3 and scarcely notices one of less than 10. Thus true acceptability can never be a fine line on any graph such as those in Figures 4.3 and 4.4. Still, reverberation conditions well outside the spectrum bands shown will produce distinct overly live or dead sound conditions.

This is a very simple view of the complex phenomenon of reverberation, for which many more variables and issues remain to be dealt with in serious design of theaters and other such places. Still, the simple reverberation time illustrated here is a major factor.

4.4 BACKGROUND NOISE

If sounds are absorbed immediately after they have been heard, the corresponding background noise levels and reverberation time may be reduced significantly. There is, however, the serious question of how much noise should be removed by absorption. That is, how quiet does one wish the room to be, or how much acoustical isolation is desirable?

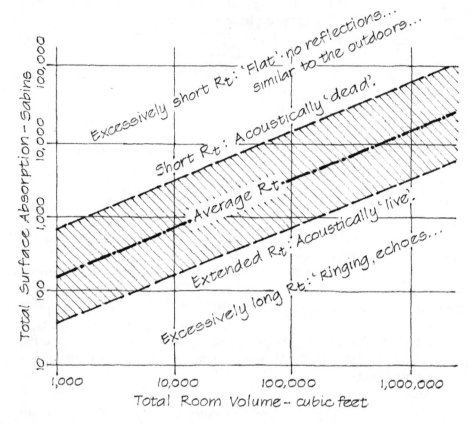

FIGURE 4.3   Reverberation related to total surface absorption and room size. Volume generally implies the size of a room, although the actual proportions of width-length-height are also of concern. A tunnel will obviously not respond the same as a cubical space. This graphic presents a very general relationship that indicates the ranges that produce an almost outdoor-like experience (very dead) on the one hand, and an echo-chamber type of response (too live) on the other extreme.

One might argue that it would be highly objectionable to reduce the background noise level to a point at which the loudest noise in a room is the scratching of a pencil by someone writing on a piece of paper. The reason for mentioning this point is to raise the issue of *acceptable* background noise. For instance, the pleasant noise of soft music might be desirable in an office if it were loud enough to render inaudible someone else's conversation but not loud enough to distract from or interfere with one's own concentration at a given task.

A common means used to reduce the potential disturbing effects of incoming noises is deliberately to add some background noise to raise the general background level, thus partly *masking* the incoming sound. Sound created for this purpose that is of a constant, single-tone nature (hum, buzz, etc.) is called *white noise*. Masking sounds of a more complex, varying form, such as music, are called *pink noise*.

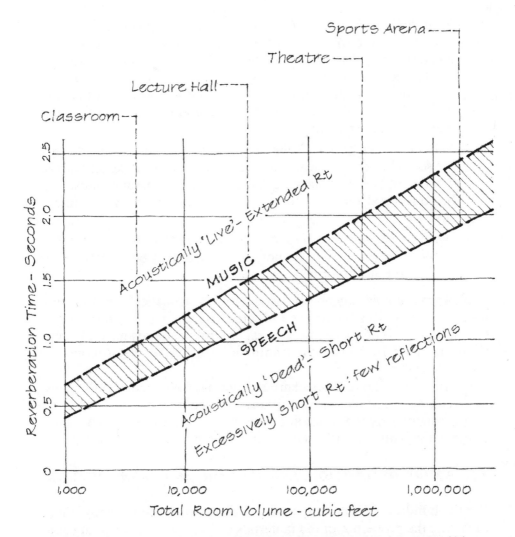

FIGURE 4.4 Reverberation effect related to reverberation time and room size. Volume is used here as in Figure 4.3 to represent room size, although the same cautions mentioned for the graph in Figure 4.3 apply here. The desirability or concern for reverberation also depends on the form of the sound and the interests or tasks of the listener. Thus what may be useful for a richer experience with orchestral music may serve to reduce audibility of human speech. This makes it difficult to perfect a room for all usage purposes, so a compromise is typically made for design unless some modifications (movable elements, etc.) are possible for different anticipated uses.

What makes background noise acceptable or unacceptable has to do with several considerations, the major one being the following:

1. *Listening Task.* What are you trying to do? Are you trying to sleep, read a book, hold a conversation, listen to a lecture, work at some task?

2. *Intensity Level of Background Noise.* Is it loud enough to be disturbing and to interfere with your listening task? In other words, are you mostly hearing the background noise and not what you want to hear (maybe nothing if you are trying to sleep or read a book)? Does it drown out the lecture? Or is it so low that it does not sufficiently mask other disturbing sounds of a particular nature, such as some-one else's conversation?

3. *Nature of the Background Noise.* There is nice, soft music and there is the screeching of a squeaky fan. There is music you like and music you do not like. Any masking sound created deliberately must also be considered for its character, not merely for its level of inten-sity.

4. *Duration of Sounds.* Either the background noise or the other sounds that you want or do not want to hear may be continuous or noncontinuous in form.

Background noise may be an issue for room acoustics if the listening task and potentially annoying sounds are all happening in a single space. Conditioning of the space and general control of sounds may all occur inside the space. In this case the manipulation of surface absorptions will be a critical design factor.

In many cases, however, background noise is most critical with regard to its relation to the potential disturbance by incoming noise, that is, noise originating outside the room and brought in by airborne or structure-borne paths. This issue is discussed in Chapter 5.

4.5 SOUND REFLECTION, ABSORPTION, AND TRANSMISSION

For the building designer, the tools for control of sound become those involving the properties of the materials employed in the building con-struction. After possibilities for manipulation of the building plans and forms have been exhausted, what remains are the choices for the selection of materials and details of the construction. This entails a concentration on the properties of the construction that most affect sound.

Reflection

Since many listeners in a room may receive most of the sound that they hear by reflection, a major concern is the nature of reflections from sur-faces. As discussed previously, major factors for reflection are the dis-tances of the reflecting surface from the sound origin and from the listener. Other significant factors are the following (see Figures 4.5 and 4.6):

Shape of the Reflecting Surface. This may be flat, convex, concave, domed or cupped, undulating, and so on. Thus the sound may be directly bounced, scattered, focused, and so on.

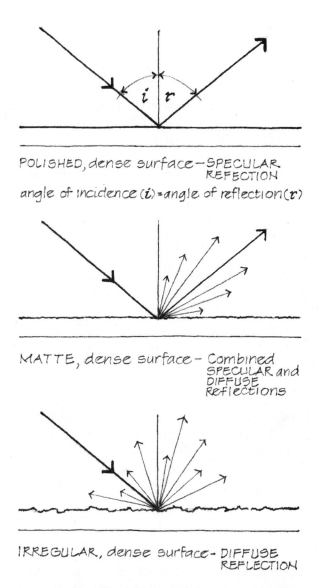

POLISHED, dense surface—SPECULAR REFECTION

angle of incidence (*i*) =angle of reflection (*r*)

MATTE, dense surface— Combined SPECULAR and DIFFUSE Reflections

IRREGULAR, dense surface- DIFFUSE REFLECTION

FIGURE 4.5 Every reflector will modify the reflected sound to some degree, which may be beneficial or may reduce audibility or lessen the purity of the sound for the listener at any given location.

Spectral Character of the Surface. The surface may be smooth, generally rough, faceted, or specially formed for selective reflections. Specific dimensions of features (bumps, grooves, holes, pleats, etc.) will relate to the size of wavelengths of specific sound frequencies.

Structural Character of the Surface. The surface may be rigid or flexible, with a particular period of fundamental vibration. It may be of very low density and be virtually porous for sound, or it may be very dense and opaque for sound transmission. An entire reflecting device or surface may be specifically "tuned" for absorption or reflection of particular sounds.

General Absorptive Character of the Surface. By various means, the surface may respond selectively to sounds of different frequencies or intensities. This may be measured at a specific frequency or evaluated for an overall response for a band of frequencies (such as those most critical for the human ear).

Techniques for control of sound available to the designer include the following:

Placement of Surfaces at Specific Locations. Floors, ceilings, walls, and any large freestanding elements within a room may be positioned with respect to each other, to the sound source, and to the listeners. These manipulations must, of course, be done in concert with the development of the user functions for the room and all the other design factors for the planning and construction.

Choices for the General Construction of the Surfaces. These will affect the various properties of general surface form, structural character, spectral character, and absorption.

It is very imiportant to establish clearly the specific goals for sound conditions in any individual space. No specific construction choice is good or bad for all purposes. As for all performance-related design, the work must begin with a thorough analysis of the desired conditions. In the end, any manipulations for sound control must be integrated with efforts made to achieve other design goals for lighting, thermal comfort, energy conservation, fire safety, and so on.

Sound Transmission

It is important to bear in mind that many of the manipulations of the construction of the enclosure of a room (floors, ceilings, and walls) must deal with issues relating to their sound transmission properties. Sound transmission most seriously affects noise control in terms of the sounds coming into a room from outside sources. This is treated more fully in Chapter 5.

The point to be made here is that the development of the construction should deal with *all* the sound control factors and behaviors that can be affected by the construction. This may be done selectively and individually for single issues such as control of reverberation time for a manageable design process, but should eventually include all the sound response issues and their consequences.

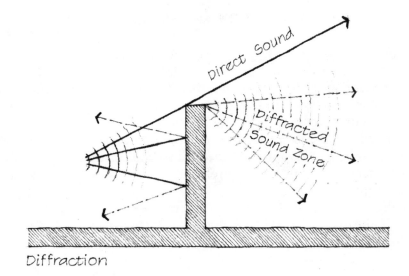

Diffraction

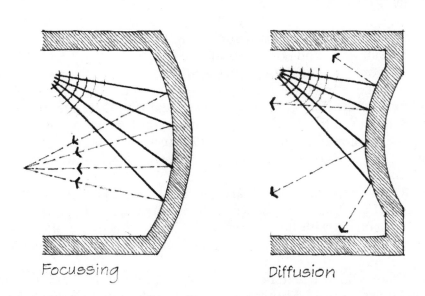

Focussing   Diffusion

FIGURE 4.6 Effects of the form of barriers in the sound pathway. Sound that wraps around an incomplete or perforated barrier undergoes diffraction that distorts the original form of the sound waves. Concave surfaces tend to produce focusing effects with reflected sounds, with the actual size or curvature of the surface relating to the dimensions of specific sound waves (at particular frequencies). Convex, bumpy, or protuberant surfaces tend to produce diffusion, or a scattering of the reflected sound waves.

4.6   SURFACE COMPOSITION AND MATERIALS

Except for some very special rooms, such as concert theaters, lecture halls, and sound recording studios, the construction of room enclosures is usually made to respond to many other concerns before sound is considered. Nevertheless, for various sound control design purposes, the properties of constructed surfaces are important. These may be selectively considered for display of data and computations for individual behaviors. The tables and graphs provided in this book give a sampling of such data presently available. Other reference sources can be pursued for much more extensive data.

In the end, however, the overall problems of design must be considered, which is the issue approached in the building case examples in Chapter 8. Within that context, illustrations of worthwhile computations for sound control are demonstrated.

4.7   INTEGRATED DESIGN

Room interior surfaces must first respond to direct user needs. Floors must be walked on and possibly be danced on, be jumped on, be driven on, and so on. They must also be frequently cleaned, possibly by extreme means such as scrubbing. Any choices for flooring as well as the structural form of the floor construction must deal with these uses, making manipulations of the floor surface the most constrained. When choices are possible, however, some major differences for sound management may be achieved by choosing among carpet, vinyl tile, hardwood blocks, or terrazzo.

Ceilings, on the other hand, are commonly the least constrained by direct use. Fred Astaire may dance on them, but most building users don't have any contact with them. However, ceiling surfaces are often quite important for lighting, so this is a major place for carefully integrated design choices.

Walls are somewhere in between floors and ceilings in regard to concerns for user contact. If quite tall, the wall surface may be divided between that within reach (up to 8 feet or so?) and that out of reach. The out-of-reach wall surface may possibly be considered in the same category with the ceiling as to vulnerability to contact wear. Like the ceiling, the upper wall surface is also important for light reflection.

Concentration on surface development may be an exercise in futility if the surfaces are not actually exposed to a considerable degree. If the floor is largely covered with furniture and people during the sound control event on which design is based, the character of the flooring may be much less significant. If a wall is mostly covered with shelves and pictures, its surface may also be insignificant. If large suspended light fixtures, signs, and decorations virtually fill a ceiling space, the ceiling surface itself may be of little note. Real usage conditions should be considered, not the condition of the uninhabited, unfurnished space.

For concerns of integrated design work, it is important to be aware of those specific issues that are critical for only singular responses and those that relate to many performance requirements. Color of room surfaces, for example, is highly critical for lighting design and aesthetic design in general but is of no real concern for sound, fire safety, thermal comfort, and many other concerns. On the other hand, the relative smoothness of a surface strongly affects reflection of sound as well as light, and may also be an issue for wear and various tactile responses of the users.

4.8 SUMMARY: DESIGN TASKS AND GOALS

Room acoustic issues can be important for any interior space. If desired sound conditions and specific listening tasks can be defined sufficiently, realistic goals can be established and translated into some particular desired performance characteristics or properties for the space in general and for the construction of surfaces.

Such an exercise should be part of the predesign effort for any building design project. Many goals may quite likely be achieved by avoiding common mistakes, by intelligent planning, or by very minor modifications of choices for basic construction, finish materials, or placement of items of building equipment. Do all the easy things first and then tackle the unavoidable problems with what you can bring to bear in acoustic expertise.

For simple, ordinary, highly repetitive cases—such as homes, schools, office buildings, stores, and restaurants—a lot of experience exists and a lot of direct help is available in useful form. Learn enough about the basic problems to be able to read the product manufacturers' brochures with some judgment and to be able to do at least the less than totally stupid basic design work.

For really complex problems—such as concert halls, sound studios, dance floors over bedrooms, and offices over bowling alleys—find the most knowledgeable and experienced acoustic consultants that you can and follow their advice.

5

SOUND AND NOISE CONTROL

Assuming the successful achievement of control of sounds within a room, the next problem to be addressed for successful control of sound is that of noise, that is, unwanted, intrusive sounds that interfere with the desired listening situation in the room. These may originate within the room, which is largely not a problem that the building designer can address; management for this is pretty much up to the building occupants. What can be addressed by the designers is sound originating somewhere else and being carried to the room by various paths. The potential for this in ordinary situations is enormous (Figure 5.1).

5.1 DEFINITION, ORIGINATION, AND CONTROL OF NOISE

The principal objective of noise control is to shield the occupants of a room from noises generated outside the space. The task of architecturally achieving acoustical privacy is becoming more and more difficult. This is due primarily to architectural trends toward lighter and more porous construction.

To ensure effective noise control, architects must consider the issue of noise during the initial design phase. A useful noise control methodology for architects may be said to consist of four sequential procedures:

1. Locate and define potential noise sources, specifically in terms of their anticipated intensities, and identify sensitive listeners.

FIGURE 5.1 Potential sources for noise in a multistory, multiunit apartment building. Sources are not all equally controllable by good building design. Those most critical for the building designer are noises from building equipment and noises transmitted between individual units (apartments and other occupied spaces). Noises within units are largely affected by the occupants and by factors relating to interior finishing and furnishings. A complete analysis for potential design concern includes considerations for pathways (airborne, structure-borne) and problems typically related to construction (leaks, crosstalk, etc.). From *A Guide to Airborne, Impact, and Structureborne Noise Control in Multifamily Dwellings* (Ref. 2).

2. Evaluate possible direct transmission paths for structure-borne as well as airborne noise.
3. Employ construction detailing, available technologies, and architectural planning to isolate and impede these various noise paths.
4. Select appropriate sound transmission class (STC)-rated and impact isolation class (IIC)-rated construction, based on the desired degree of attenuation between spaces.

Noise Sources

Perhaps the single most important rule to learn regarding noise control is that the best (and often the only) place to control noise effectively is at its source. Once noise has radiated throughout a building, its control requires large amounts of design ingenuity, technology, and money. Even then, the design solution may be only partially successful, especially if it depends critically on modifications of basic structures or performance of unusual construction. Whenever and wherever possible, one should isolate and control the noise at the point of origin.

Noise sources abound in any situation (see Figure 5.1). Some are obvious and easily identified and located (noisy fans, flushing toilets, slamming of heavy doors). Others may be more elusive and emerge only after completion of the construction (gurgling of water in drain pipes, whistling of air in ducts, harmonic vibration of objects due to ordinary sources of vibrations).

For all identifiable sources—or even strongly suspected ones—some anticipation should be planned for in the design. Desired goals should be given to all members of the design team for acoustic properties of equipment and components of the building construction.

A particularly difficult problem is one that occurs when the basic building design contract does not include the work for the complete design of interior spaces. This happens commonly in commercial office and retail facilities, where the final development of interiors is done by individual designers and contractors, often employed by the tenants. This work can include all interior finishes as well as ceilings and partition walls. That includes a lot of what matters for room acoustics and noise control.

At issue here is the fact that a potential noise source may not be a problem at all if there are relatively easy means for blocking its paths to potential listeners. If the designer can be assured of having control of the paths, the potential source may be ignored in terms of modification at the source. However, when the paths are subject to change or to other designer's decisions, it is best to deal with the problem at the source, leaving the other factors out of the picture and free of acoustic concern.

Noise Paths

To achieve the goal of effective noise control architects must understand and appreciate the paths that noise may take through a building. There are basically two paths that noise (and sound in general) may take. The first is through the air, and the second is through the structure of a building. Designers should take note that the control of airborne noise is by far easier than the control of structure-borne noise. Basically, once any path is identified through evaluation of the construction, what is required is that the sound path be blocked by some means.

In terms of airborne noise control, the physical behavior of sound must be reemphasized. Airborne noise will enter a space through any opening it is afforded, regardless of the size, shape, or location of the opening (Figure 5.2). Among the more common openings through the solid construction are those deliberately created for HVAC ducts, electrical wiring, piping, and wall-recessed fixtures such as electrical switches and outlets, phone and cable TV jacks, hose cabinets, and bathroom cabinets.

Ordinary construction practices also result in gaps and cracks that are sufficient to serve as sound leaks. These occur at all edges of walls surfaced with drywall materials and around windows and doors. Many sound leaks can be plugged in the same manner as is done for air leaks in the building exterior envelope: by caulking (Figure. 5.3). Caulking materials are elastic and resilient and will stick to surfaces and plug holes in almost any type of construction.

Operable windows may be weather-proofed to some degree (made airtight), but doors must be loose to some degree in order to open easily. Ceiling plenums that are continuous over partition walls and pipe chases that run from floor to floor are also potential channeled conduits for sound. The attainment of any degree of airborne noise control must begin with the effective blocking of these openings.

Structure-borne noise is by far the most difficult to control. This is due in part to the speed with which sound travels through solids. The velocity of sound in air is approximately 1130 feet per second, while its velocity through stone, for instance, is about 12,000 feet per second. In addition, once sound has entered a structure, the only way to block its path is literally to break the structural continuity. Every separation has the potential to impede the path of structure-borne sound.

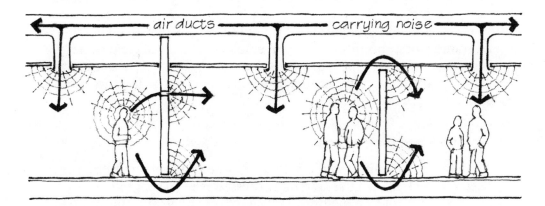

FIGURE 5.2 Airborne noise paths. Airborne noise that is incoming to a space may travel through relatively sound-transparent barriers (with low STC). However, the more common situations involve travel through leaks in the barriers, by flanking around the barriers, or through sound channels such as connecting ducts, corridors, pipe chases, elevator shafts, stairways, or other continuous passageways.

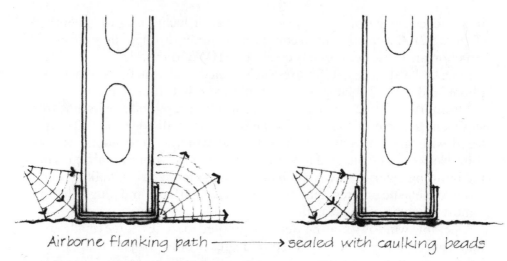

Airborne flanking path ─────────────→ sealed with caulking beads

FIGURE 5.3 Ordinary construction tolerances and situations result in various problems for sound control. Wood sills or sheet metal sills (shown here) are never perfectly fit to their supports, leaving considerable potential for sound leaks in spite of superior acoustic performance of the developed wall surfaces and wall construction as a barrier. Leaks can be effectively closed by simple caulking between the sill and the support. Wall ends or tops abutting other structures may receive the same treatment.

The only effective way of controlling structure-borne noise may be to isolate the source and prevent its initial entry into the structure (Figure 5.4). Isolation may be achieved by structural separation within the path but can also be achieved by placing the source at a remote location. However, sound can travel with great efficiency for long distances through many structures, so this is not as effective a means as for airborne noises.

Where possible, discontinuous structural systems, which do not transfer sound vibrations from one member to the next, are of great value (see Figure 5.5). However, most widely used concrete and steel structures have considerable continuity, so that other means must be used to control structure-borne sounds.

Attenuation of the Enclosure

Assuming that all direct sound paths (airborne and structure-borne) have been blocked, the next area to be addressed is of special interest to the architect—the role the enclosure system plays in preventing the intrusion of noise into the room. This factor deals with how much reduction in the transmission of noise may be expected of the walls, floor, and ceiling of any room. The tendency of the enclosure system to reduce sound is referred to as the *sound attenuation* property of construction.

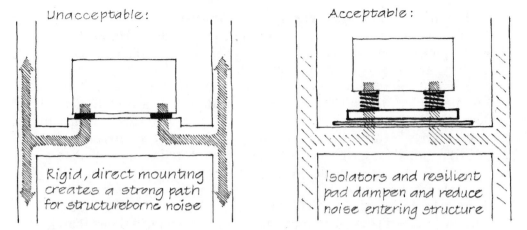

FIGURE 5.4 Structure-borne noise. The main culprit for structure-borne noise is building equipment that is rigidly connected (coupled) to the structure. Any vibration of the equipment (as sound or simply as violent shaking) will be broadcast efficiently throughout the continuous structure and much of the rest of the construction that is rigidly attached (coupled) to it. If the offending equipment cannot be quieted, it should be decoupled from the structure by a vibration-separating attachment. Otherwise, or possibly in addition, the structure itself should be decoupled in units to reduce continuity throughout the building, or other elements (walls, floors, ceilings) should be decoupled from the structure.

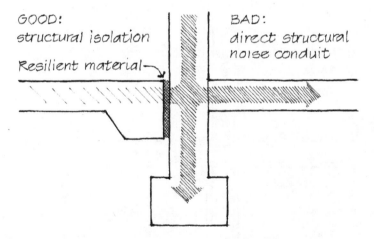

FIGURE 5.5 Ordinary construction joints often produce sufficient structural continuity to transmit structure-borne sounds with considerable efficiency (little loss of energy in the transmission). Breaking the continuity is helpful; doing it with an energy-absorbing joint filler is best.

The question facing designers is twofold: first, how much sound attenuation is feasible, and second, how much is desirable? The answers to these questions are predicated on human comfort criteria for acoustical privacy, available construction technologies, and associated costs. Decisions are made by evaluating potential sources of noise and their associated intensities and by establishing the desired or acceptable sound levels for the given space and its activities (Figure 5.6). The difference in sound levels between the two will govern the *sound transmission class* (STC) required for the given enclosure. The STC rating of any construction simply describes the theoretical amount of noise reduction in decibels that may be expected. Due to the variability of construction practices, it is advisable to specify an STC rating higher than that actually required. Due to common construction practices, it is prudent to assume that the true value of the STC for a rated construction will be at least 5 *dB* lower than that established in a controlled laboratory situation.

The principal factors that govern the STC rating of any construction component are material weight, mass, and rigidity. The greater the weight, mass, and rigidity, the greater the corresponding attenuation produced. The attenuation value increases by almost 5 dB for every doubling of the weight (per square foot) of the construction. A drop of 5 *dB* is a per-

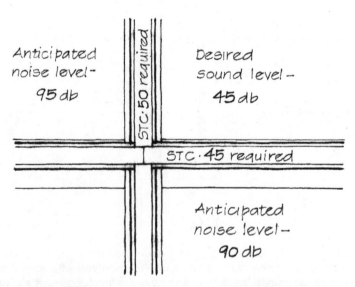

FIGURE 5.6   Use of STC values for barriers. The simple, direct purpose of the quantified STC value for a barrier is in evaluating its effectiveness for reduction of airborne noise levels between building spaces. This requires an estimation of the level of the noise source and the establishment of a target value for the background noise level in the affected space. The minimum value for the STC of a barrier is thus determined as the simple difference of sound levels on the two sides of the barrier. Individual cases require other considerations, but this is the simple use of the STC value.

ceptible and significant reduction in the loudness of a sound, so the effectiveness of density increase should not be under-valued. This illustrates the difficulties in achieving acoustical privacy in buildings that employ lightweight construction. The basis for STC ratings and their use for design are discussed more fully in Section 5.4.

5.2 ACCEPTABLE BACKGROUND NOISE

The issue of background noise is discussed in Chapter 4 with regard to the listening and communication tasks within a room. In the typical situation, what constitutes background noise is some combination of sounds that originate within the room and those incoming as noise from outside the room enclosure. In the end, the listener has a singular experience and the source of the background noise is of little note; only its intensity level and general nature matter for any listening tasks.

Acceptable background levels are highly subjective and have much to do with the conditioned responses and hearing capabilities of the listener. Extreme levels of noise, such as that experienced by standing next to a loud source such as a screaming steam whistle, will pretty much wipe out any hearing possibilities. However, acute hearing can depend as much on the listener's ability to concentrate and to isolate selective sounds as on any measured intensities or frequencies.

Goals for background noise to be used for design criteria must first consider the listener's desired situation. Is it to be able to hear something? Possibly a lecture, music, another person speaking in conversation, or someone on the other end of a phone line. In this case any background noise must be considered as potential interference with the task, whether it is sound originating in the same room or incoming noise. A basic design goal therefore is to reduce the level of the background noise below that of the desired sound being listened to.

However, the nature of the ambient background noise must also be considered. Is it of a high level in the same frequency band as the sound being concentrated on? Is it generally intense in the range most critical for the human ear? Is it of the same nature (voice, music) as what the listener is trying to concentrate on? Even low-level background noises may be distracting if they have a particular character. If you hate Bach, it is not going to be comfortable to have it as background "noise."

A special situation is presented in the case of the listener who is really trying *not* to hear: for example, someone trying to sleep. In this case, a background level of some reasonable intensity, consisting of relatively soothing sounds, may be desirable. It may be a means for masking intrusive, potentially disturbing sounds.

If the real listening task can be defined successfully in these terms, one may proceed with considerations for exercising controls on the background noise. Typically, these must include some items that relate to sound control within the room and some that relate to the control of incoming noise.

For any custom design of the room enclosure (walls, floors, roofs, doors), it is necessary to establish a specific value for the acceptable (or maybe desirable) background noise level. Juggling of the sound-attenuating properties for the enclosing construction cannot be done without some target for attenuation of the sound transmissions. Code requirements and general guidelines for particular occupancies may stipulate minimum recommended values, but they are based on somebody's assumption of what is considered to be an acceptable noise level.

5.3   REVERBERATION AND BACKGROUND NOISE

Background noise does not qualify as such unless it is enduring over time. Few situations involve background noise levels that are uniformly continuous, so an average is assumed for the reference background noise level for design. Enduring sounds are produced by sources that are continuous (running fan, etc.) or by sources that involve continuing repetitions (people conversing, etc.).

If a room has a large amount of hard, dense, reflective surfaces, it will have an extended reverberation time and a considerable probability for high levels of ambient background noise; this is described for acoustical purposes as being very *live.* Conversely, if a room contains porous, soft, absorptive surfaces, it will have a short reverberation time, low levels of background noise, and will be described as *dead.* In an enclosed space, part of what creates an enduring sound condition is reverberation time. If the room is excessively "live," continuing sounds can merge into a resonant howling or ringing effect. (See the discussion of reverbation in Section 4.3.)

While dealing wtih room acoustics may be separated from dealing with incoming noises for investigation or design, the two effects eventually join for a single experience by listeners. Measurements of listener responses and performance data for sound sources, isolation mechanisms, attenuating enclosures, or reflecting surfaces must relate eventually to the combined, simultaneous experience of listeners. Considerations for reverberation, speech audibility, echoes, and other concerns must recognize this entire sensation for affected spaces and listeners.

5.4   SOUND PRIVACY

Sound privacy for an affected listener may be provided by the reduction of sound transmission and the achievement of a desired degree of sound isolation. All means possible are available for the reduction, and the most effective means depends on many factors regarding the circumstances (Figure 5.7).

Sound Insulation

An effective means for reduction of sound transmission is to place some form of *sound insulation* between the source and the listener. This works essentially the same as thermal insulation, reducing the flow of energy from sender to receiver in some quantified differential below which it would be without the interception. As with thermal flow, one visualizes a certain drop in sound energy level through the barrier, indicating its insulative value.

By their very definition, acoustically absorbent materials will allow sound energy to enter the material, and perhaps allow it to pass through, but will severely reduce the amount of sound reflected (see Figure 5.8). They are soft and porous and may be quite nonelastic in their behavior. Sounds will lose their energy before they are reflected back into a space. Think of trying to play handball where the surface the ball strikes is soft, porous, and hangs away from the wall (like a heavy velour curtain) so that it moves backwards when the ball strikes it. Successful absorbents by their very nature will probably not be good insulators by themselves, although absorbent materials within a wall cavity may moderate the sound transmission through the whole wall assembly.

Insulating potential can be determined for various materials (wood, plaster, glass, etc.), but the more practical measurement is something like the STC or IIC value as determined for an entire barrier element. Factors must be included for various details of the installation of the construction (edge seals, treatments of joints, etc.) as well as the basic materials of the barrier.

Sound Isolation

Insulation may be one means for achieving a more general condition described as *sound isolation*. This refers to the interception of energy flow by isolating either the source or the listener, or possibly both. The properties of effective sound isolating materials are opposite to those of absorbents; they are heavy, hard, dense, and rigid (see Figure 5.8). As the sound reaches the isolating surface it is mostly reflected, partially absorbed, and almost none is transmitted through the barrier. Playing handball against this type of surface will be a pretty active experience.

Isolation can be achieved by other means, including creating a separating distance, deflection or diffraction of direct transmissions, decoupling, or otherwise breaking of the continuity of a structure or any continuous transmission pathway such as piping or HVAC ducts.

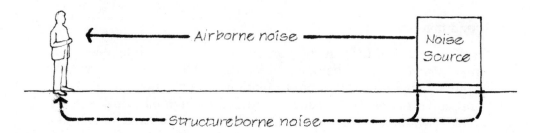

a. WORST SITUATION — NO ISOLATION

Airborne noise

Noise Source

Structureborne noise

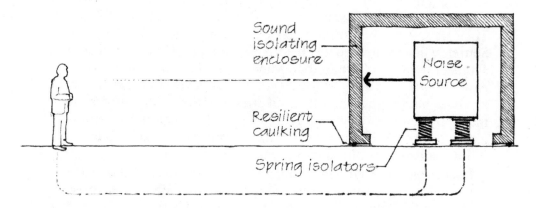

b. BEST SITUATION — ISOLATION OF SOURCE

Sound isolating enclosure

Noise Source

Resilient caulking

Spring isolators

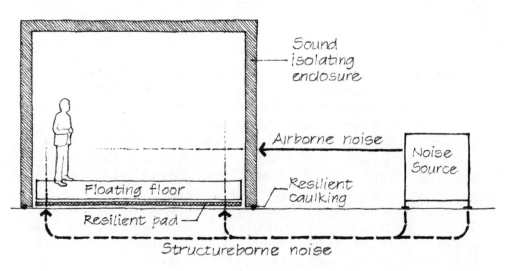

c. ACCEPTABLE SITUATION — ISOLATION OF LISTENER

Sound isolating enclosure

Airborne noise

Noise Source

Floating floor

Resilient caulking

Resilient pad

Structureborne noise

An insulative enclosure for either the source or the listener. Isolation of the source is indicated if a single source affects a number of listeners or building spaces. This will be particularly effective if structure-borne noises are critical and the source can be isolated from the structure to a significant degree (see Figure 5.9). If airborne sounds from the source are critical, and distance cannot be used effectively to reduce transmission, a sound-attenuating enclosure (heavily insulated) may be a solution.

Isolation of the listener may be best if only selected sensitive spaces occur in a single building and they are affected by many sources. It is relatively easy to isolate a single sensitive space if the main problem is airborne sound and the space is already enclosed by construction. Part of the construction as planned may be sufficient and other parts can be altered or enhanced to obtain the necessary level of insulation or energy-flow separation. Of course, attention must also be paid to all possible leaks and flanking.

Isolation of sensitive spaces is somewhat more difficult where structure-borne vibrations are a major problem. It is a challenge to develop total enclosure for an interior building space and have all the enclosing construction decoupled from the structure. It might be done, but it usually requires some very special construction, notably for attachment and support of the enclosing walls, floor, and ceiling. It is smart to exhaust all other possibilities for mitigation of the noise and vibrations before attempting to isolate the affected space.

5.5 MEANS FOR ACHIEVING SOUND AND NOISE CONTROL

Means available to the building designer for the control of sound include manipulation of ordinary architectural and construction design factors and the possible use of special modifications that make use of technology that is specifically developed for sound control. Following is a summary of the generally available means for design control of sound, grouped under three categories: architectural design, construction development, and special means.

FIGURE 5.7 Obtaining sound privacy: insulation versus isolation. The basic problem for sound privacy is the separation of a sound source from an affected listener. The basic means for modificatioin are to suppress the source, protect the listener, or somehow modify the transmission path. One solution is to wrap either the source or the listener in an insulated (sound attenuated) enclosure: walls and floors with high STC, no leaks, and so on. However, the basic concept is one of isolation, concentrating on basically removing either the source or the listener from participation in the sound action. Isolation may thus utilize any available means, possibly including concentration on the path mechanisms, not the source or listener. Just possibly, every available means will be used for really critical cases.

a. INSULATION

Incident Sound

Absorption

Absorption

Little or no Reflection

Strong Transmission

Material Characteristics

- porous
- fibrous
- absorptive
- flaccid
- lightweight

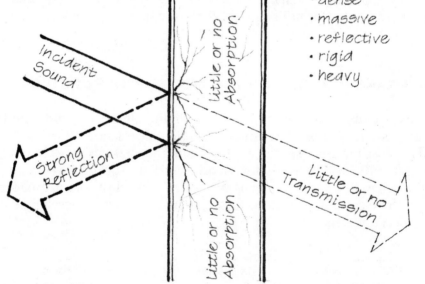

b. ISOLATION

Incident Sound

Little or no Absorption

Little or no Absorption

Strong Reflection

Little or no Transmission

Material Characteristics

- dense
- massive
- reflective
- rigid
- heavy

FIGURE 5.8 Low density, porous insulating materials may serve well as sound absorbers to create reduction of reflected sounds, but they do little for reduction of transmission through the material. Inside a hollow wall assemblage they may serve a purpose, however, if the assemblage is otherwise considerably resistive to transmission. In general, the strong isolating barrier is hard, rigid, and dense.

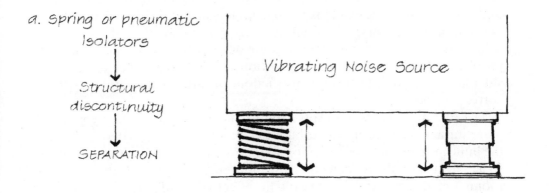

a. Spring or pneumatic
   Isolators
         ↓
   Structural
   discontinuity
         ↓
   SEPARATION

Vibrating Noise Source

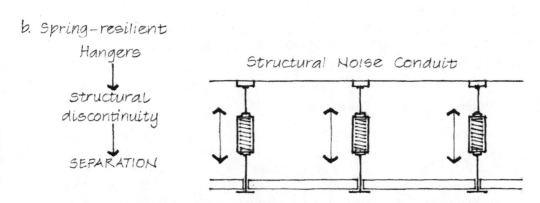

b. Spring-resilient
   Hangers
         ↓
   structural
   discontinuity
         ↓
   SEPARATION

Structural Noise Conduit

FIGURE 5.9 Isolation of the source of structure-borne noise. Ideal is the direct separation of the source itself from the structure with energy-absorbing support devices. If direct separation of the source is not possible, a discontinuity within the structure-borne path may be possible, essentially isolating one part of the structure from the other. The latter method may focus on the affects on individual spaces or listeners.

Architectural Design Options

The most successful way to control noise in buildings is to avoid creating situations that lead to acoustical defects in the programming, planning, and initial design phases. This may be largely accomplished by careful evaluation of ordinary, commonly-occurring problems; situations that informed designers should be well aware of. Early attention to common problems often results in the elimination of most later necessary considerations for architectural, construction, or structural techniques to correct defects.

The first and best way to solve sound and noise problems: by good planning and basic design of the building. Basic arrangement of spaces in the building can avoid potential problems of adjacency (quiet and noisy spaces next or or above each other), locations of major noise sources (fan rooms, toilets, gymnasiums, etc.) and the effective use of potential buffers such as stairs, corridors, and storage rooms. Besides all the other design factors, sound control should be somewhere in the criteria for basic layout of the building.

In addition to basic planning, locations of items of the construction and equipment that relate critically to sound problems should be noted. This includes windows, doors, wall-recessed fixtures, ducts, pipe chases, and all equipment that potentially generates noise and/or sensible vibrations. Shapes of rooms and individual interior surfaces should be considered for their effects on reverberations, channeling, directed reflections, focusing, and so on.

Development of the Construction

Careful planning and choices for construction may make the achieving of some sound control goals feasible. The earlier in the design process that this is recognized, the less trouble it will cause for the designers. Technology can only accomplish so much. If the cost of special work or the likelihood for construction management control is out of reach, planning and choices for basic construction must be used to achieve any sound control goals.

The basic forms, materials, and details used for exterior walls, floor and roof structures, ceilings, and interior partitions will establish a basis from which any necessary modifications, additions, or special technology for sound control must be developed.

For room acoustics the primary attention is on surface forms and finishes. This may be an area of limited control by the building designers, since interiors are often developed both initially and in any future occupancy changes by other designers. However, *whoever* does the design, attention should be given to the sound-absorbing properties of finish materials and to general sound-reflecting characteristics of the elements that form the room interiors.

Once the basic planning is done and the basic forms of construction are established, the needs for affected spaces can determine some evaluation criteria for sound properties of the construction. STC, IIC, isolation, and other potentials should be identified and options for necessary modifications should be explored. Practicality of development of attenuated enclosures and of controlling the broadcast of structure-borne sounds should be investigated.

Where special construction is desired, it must be recognized that special effort must be made to see that it happens. This starts with good construction drawings and specifications but must include adequate inspection of the construction work. Workers develop routines for accomplishing ordinary construction, and if you are asking for something else, you had better be sure it actually happens.

Special Techniques and Methods for Sound Control

Once all the initial options for planning and development of the basic construction are exhausted and sound control goals have still not been reached, various possibilities for special work (design and/or construction) must be considered. In general, these include the following:

Increased Insulative Values. Flow of sound energy through enclosing barriers can be reduced by various means, including the addition of insulative elements or changes in such basic materials as wall paneling and floor decks.

Special Installation. Ordinary materials may be installed with some special consideration or extra elements to improve sound behavior (see Figure 5.10). Some manufacturers will provide recommen-

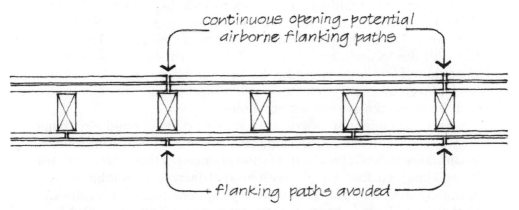

FIGURE 5.10 Modifications of ordinary construction. First attention should be given to simple procedures or details that do not involve additions or changes of basic materials. When surfaces are developed in layers, leaks may be reduced by staggering the joints in the separate layers, which should not add any cost to the construction.

dations for modifications of the installation of their products, with associated levels of effectiveness in the levels of sound absorption or transmission. The drywall-surfaced, stud-framed partition is endlessly modifiable in this regard (see the Appendix).

Use of Isolation Devices. Special elements may be used within the construction to intercept, dampen, or absorb vibrations. This includes the use of sound-control matting in floors, resilient furring channels for wall paneling, and absorbing separators between supporting or connecting elements of the construction (wall to wall, wall to floor, etc.).

Surface Modifications. This includes special plaster, tiles, fabrics, and various materials chosen particularly for their sound-reflecting characteristics.

Deliberate Creation of Sound. This refers primarily to the possible use of white or pink noise to modify background sound levels, as discussed in Section 4.4.

Ordinary problems generally have ordinary and obvious solutions—not always, easy, practical, or feasible solutions, but ones that should be obvious to informed designers. Special problems call for some more professional expertise, and the best available should be obtained. Clever and experienced acoustic specialists may be able to dig from a large bag of tricks to solve special problems. Still, the previous admonition regarding the likelihood of actually obtaining well-executed special construction should be noted.

5.6 EXTERIOR NOISE SOURCES

Noises entering the building from outside include those generated on and off the building site. Management of the interior/exterior site-to-building sound interchange should be subject to some design effort. These may deal with the locating or enclosure of any noisy exterior equipment, separation of buildings in groups, location of noisy site activities (children's playgrounds, etc.), or use of site planting or site construction (walls, earth forms) to achieve some separation.

Noises incoming from heavily traveled streets, other buildings, flying aircraft, or other off-site sources cannot usually be controlled at the sources, which leaves basically the efforts of good planning or the enhancement of the building's enclosing shell. With an ever-increasing amount of new construction occurring in crowded urban locations, this form of enhancement for buildings is becoming almost a routine situation. Ordinary forms of wall construction and the construction elements used to achieve enclosure are rated for acoustic transmission and respect is paid to this value in many designs.

In many buildings windows are a principal source of entry for exterior sounds. Many of the efforts made to achieve good weather seals or thermal response also improve resistance to sound transmission, which helps to reinforce choices justified previously only for HVAC considerations. Use of laminated and double glazing is of particular note in this regard, especially for multistory office buildings, where the percentage of glazed wall surface is usually quite high.

Where low-flying air traffic is considerable, the sound barrier effect of roofs becomes important, especially for low-rise buildings where the roof surface may constitute a major portion of the total building enclosure. The whole sandwich of roofing, insulation, structure, interstitial space, and ceiling must be analyzed for this total effect, making for many possible variations to enhance the construction.

Site planning and landscaping options can be used to at least reduce the impact of externally generated noises. While plant materials are generally transparent to sound, they do affect the reflecting properties of the ground surface. Sound will bounce much more efficiently from a paved surface than from one covered with grass or other plantings. Creating a rolling surface with plant-covered earth berms will produce acoustical shadows, as well as create a visual sensation that may serve a psychological function to reduce the impact of the sound experience for listeners (see Figure 5.11).

Situations for exterior noise are very special events, affected by many factors. The really noisy urban setting may represent a potential for overwhelming external noise. However, once one becomes adjusted to it—and possibly less annoyed from long experience with the situation—it can have the possibility of providing a high level of background noise to

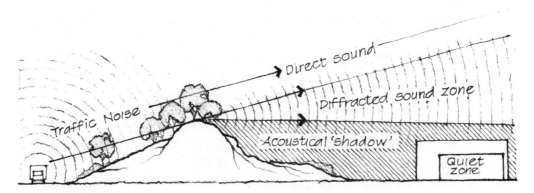

FIGURE 5.11 Where possible, site planning may be able to create some quiet zones by acoustic blocking or shadows. There are various scale effects here that relate to the actual dimensions of the site and the form of the sound waves with most potential for disturbing listeners. Individual tricks may therefore be most effective only for particular noise sources.

mask other potentially disturbing sounds. The quiet country setting may be very peaceful, but being able to hear a pin drop in the night may be a highly vulnerable condition.

Obviously one of the most effective defenses against intruding external noises is to tightly seal the building envelope. This has also been chosen as a means of maintaining a highly controlled building interior for other reasons in the past. Presently, however, there is a lot of concern for the loss of natural ventilation and the potential for a "sick" interior with various internally-generated toxic conditions. This is a very sensitive area, requiring careful ranking of values and goals before any optimizing of design is undertaken.

5.7   SUMMARY: PROBLEMS AND DESIGN GOALS

The following is a summary of considerations for sound and noise control as related to the building design process.

1. Evaluate potential noise sources. Identify all the possible sources for noise and determine any actual data for the sound output. Data should include considerations of intensity (loudness), singular or dominant frequencies, form or structure of the sound, and duration. Evaluate the potential for noise distribution paths from the sources throughout the building by all possible airborne or structure-borne pathways. Consider the possibilities for control of the noise at the source by choice of the noise-generating elements or by modifications of installation or construction details.

2. Determine all sound-sensitive spaces in the building with regard to hearing tasks or sound privacy in general. Establish specific data for desired goals for affected spaces and derive desired properties for sound-attenuating elements of the construction. Be sure to consider any direct relationships between listening tasks and the nature of intruding noises—for example, other conversations will disturb your conversation more than traffic noise.

3. Use basic planning of the building and the site, location of noise-generating sources, and positioning of windows, doors, corridors, and other elements to achieve sound control goals. Identify spaces that are fixed in location and thus placed in special jeopardy for sound control problems, indicating need for special design efforts.

4. Identify spaces with multiple tasks regarding sound conditions and develop priorities or generalized data for achieving the best sound situations for all uses. Consider possibilities for user-manipulatable elements for modification of sound conditions for different uses in a single space.

5. Evaluate all situations likely to require the use of acoustic design consultation. If specific heightened client expectations or aspirations for special sound quality environments exist, expert advice is highly indicated. Don't try to solve anything but routine problems on your own.

6

CONTROL OF AIRBORNE NOISE

In this chapter we treat the issue of airborne sounds, considered as intrusive to an enclosed space (room). The emphasis is on what can be done in the form of building planning or development of the construction to reduce the problems.

6.2 PLANNING CONSIDERATIONS

A primary consideration for airborne noise is distance from the source. Unless it is highly channeled by a structured pathway such as an air duct or long corridor, airborne sound tends to fall off in intensity very rapidly as the distance from the source is increased. This leads to a principal effort in planning, which is the simple dimensional separation of source and listeners.

Placing a potentially annoying source (fan room, toilet, music room, shop, etc.) as far away as possible from listeners likely to be disturbed is rule number one. To the extent that this can be achieved within the feasible alternative plan options, it presents the most effective planning action for noise control, and unusually the least expensive.

The second most important item is the elimination of sound pathways. Do everything possible to reduce the potential for direct sound, major reflections, flanking, leaks, crosstalk, and all the easy means of travel for the airborne sound.

If other planning objectives make it necessary to place a potential noise source immediately adjacent to the room with listeners, plan the general construction to make it possible to provide the most effective barrier between the adjacent building spaces. Allow for the dimensions and details necessary for really sound-resistive construction. Avoid having to penetrate the solid construction with ducts, piping, and wiring as much as possible. Place doors and windows to make flanking and leaks the least likely to occur.

6.2   SOURCES AND PATHS

Preceding any planning effort, of course, is the necessity to identify potential noise sources. Ordinary sources, such as fans and flushing of toilets, occur in most buildings. Other sources may relate to the size or special uses of a building, possibly involving items such as large refrigeration units, elevators, loud music, or sports activities.

Noises can exist and not be a problem, of course, if there is nobody listening who might be disturbed. Identifying *problem noises*, therefore, includes some identification of the potentially annoyed parties. Noises occur in just about all buildings (noisy equipment, slamming doors, people talking and yelling, etc.). Define a particular occupancy and there will be both special noise sources and defined listening situations. See Figure 5.1 for all the possible bad situations in multiunit housing.

The paths of travel of the sound must also be identified. For some noises this may be primarily an airborne path and for others primarily a structure-borne path. Airborne sound may be direct, be reflected, or be channeled through connecting spaces (hallways, ducts, pipe chases). It may come from flanking around or leaks through a barrier (Figure 6.1). Typically, however, many common noises are transmitted by some combination of pathways.

For full effectiveness, all pathways should be dealt with; however, the most significant ones need some concentration. The main culprit, for example, may be one particular pathway, and dealing with that may produce sufficient modification if the total transmission from other paths is tolerable.

6.3   TECHNIQUES FOR CONTROL

Control of noise may be achieved effectively by a single effort or by a combination of several efforts. Considered individually, the principal efforts include the following:

FLANKING NOISE PATHS

F1. OPEN PLENUMS OVER WALLS, FALSE CEILINGS
F2 UNBAFFLED DUCT RUNS
F3 OUTDOOR PATH, WINDOW TO WINDOW
F4 CONTINUOUS UNBAFFLED INDUCTOR UNITS
F5 HALL PATH, OPEN VENTS
F6 HALL PATH, LOUVERED DOORS
F7 HALL PATH, OPENINGS UNDER DOORS
F8 OPEN TROUGHS IN FLOOR-CEILING STRUCTURE

NOISE LEAKS

L1 POOR SEAL AT CEILING EDGES
L2 POOR SEAL AROUND DUCT PENETRATIONS
L3 POOR MORTAR JOINTS, POROUS MASONRY BLK
L4 POOR SEAL AT SIDEWALL, FILLER PANEL ETC.
L5 BACK TO BACK CABINETS, POOR WORKMANSHIP
L6 HOLES, GAPS AT WALL PENETRATIONS
L7 POOR SEAL AT FLOOR EDGES
L8 BACK TO BACK ELECTRICAL OUTLETS
L9 HOLES, GAPS AT FLOOR PENETRATIONS

OTHER POINTS TO CONSIDER, RE: LEAKS ARE (A) BATTEN STRIP A/O POST CONNECTIONS OF PREFABRICATED WALLS, (B) UNDER FLOOR PIPE OR SERVICE CHASES, (C) RECESSED, SPANNING LIGHT FIXTURES, (D) CEILING & FLOOR COVER PLATES OF MOVABLE WALLS, (E) UNSUPPORTED A/O UNBACKED WALL BOARD JOINTS (F) EDGES & BACKING OF BUILT-IN CABINETS & APPLIANCES, (G) PREFABRICATED, HOLLOW METAL, EXTERIOR CURTAIN WALLS.

FIGURE 6.1 Paths for airborne noise. Buildings are complex in form and in the details of the construction. Eliminating all the possible paths for noise is a major effect. In most cases it is more effective to concentrate on those that are most critical; however, this may mean actually trying to visualize all the conceivable paths first in order to make the evaluation as to which are most important to worry about. From *A Guide to Airborne, Impact, and Structureborne Noise Control in Multifamily Dwellings* (Ref. 2).

Isolate or Mitigate the Source

Eliminate or reduce the intensity of the noise—buy a quiet fan instead of a noisy one. Control the noise once it is generated—enclose the fan to the degree possible in a sound-attenuating enclosure: a sealed space or a containing wrap or hood. Locate the source in the building as far away as possible from listeners likely to be annoyed. Place doors, windows, corridors, open stairs, or other pathway devices so as to reduce airborne transmissions to sensitive spaces as much as possible.

Condition the Pathways

For any pathways that cannot effectively be eliminated, do what is possible to make them the least efficient. Intercept the direct paths with barriers even if they are not airtight; change the path from primarily direct to primarily reflected or otherwise indirect. Use highly absorbent surfaces or articulate a formed surface to reduce the intensity level of reflections or to avoid bouncing them directly to some undesired location. Place and form reflecting surfaces in general so as to aim the sound away from listeners.

Condition the Listening Space

Manipulate the background noise to mask the potentially annoying incoming noise. This may be a simple arithmetic exercise (juggling decibels and STCs as shown in Figure 5.4) or may relate to the form of the noise and the type of source. Masking a steady whine from a fan or the complex sounds of traffic from a busy street is different from masking incoming voices. What *kind* of background noise exists may be as important as its level. Voices tend to command one's attention with an instinctive urge to understand what is being said.

Techniques, technology, and clever design in general can achieve a lot. Product manufacturers have all sorts of items for selection. Acoustic specialists have large bags of tricks. What is important is to know what *ought to be done*, specific goals that are realistic and can be defined, and the most effective, low-cost, easily executed means for achieving the goals.

6.4 CONSTRUCTION SOLUTIONS FOR AIRBORNE NOISE

In general, sound control methods that require any expensive modifications or additions to the building construction should be a last resort. Mitigation of noise sources, elimination of pathways by good planning, and other cost-free means should be fully exhausted first. Only after all of that if the goals are still not met should behaviors related to the construction be considered.

The objectives that may be realized by modifications of the construction are the following:

Modified Reflections

This relates to considerations for reverberation time and background noise and efforts to achieve sound reinforcement. A principal factor is the surfacing material of the reflecting surface. However, the total area and shape of the reflector (flat, concave, convex, pleated, etc.) and the entire nature of the construction of the reflecting structure (stud wall, concrete wall, etc.) may be critical.

Significance and effectiveness of modifications depend on the type of sound and the task of the listeners. Very specific performance requirements should be defined for any modification. What needs to be accomplished? Is it shortening of reverberation time, absorbing of a particular frequency of sound, redirection of the sound pathway, or some other objective?

Reduction of Transmissions

Construction modification may result in a reduction in the level of transmitted sound: generating a higher STC for the barrier. Assuming the barrier to be intact (no leaks) and the barrier itself to be more important than flanking paths or other problems, this is a primary means for improving conditions.

This may be achieved at little or no extra cost if attention is simply paid to the sound-transmission properties of the various feasible alternatives for ordinary construction of the barriers. Additions or modifications can always be made, but one should start with the best choice for the basic construction in the first place.

Elimination of Generic Faults

This refers to faults that relate to sound transmission, not necessarily to errors in the construction. Commonly used details of ordinary construction create many possible leaks for sound. Before considering changes in the basic construction, the effectiveness and feasibility of improving on the basic construction should be considered. Caulking under the sill and around all the edges of a gypsum drywall partition can result in a dramatic drop in transmitted sound simply by reducing the leaks (see Figure 6.2).

Even if major changes are made in the basic construction, these measures should also be included. Using double layers of the drywall and resilient furring may add up for an STC analysis, but if the leaks are still there, it may not really do its job.

a. Standard single-ply construction.

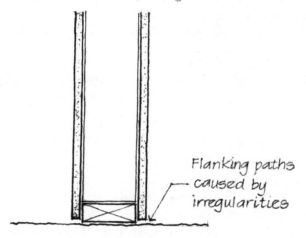

Flanking paths
caused by
irregularities

b. Standard stud with 2-ply construction,
caulking beads to seal leaks caused by
irregularities providing unseen flanking paths.

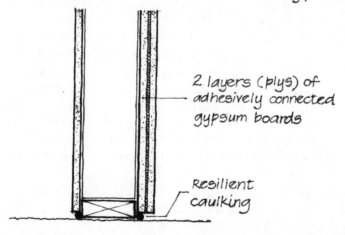

2 layers (plys) of
adhesively connected
gypsum boards

Resilient
caulking

FIGURE 6.2 Variations of basic stud construction. Two modifications are shown here: caulking of the edges of the basic wall sheathing (at ends and tops, as well as at the sill as shown here), and adding a second layer of surface panelling to create a much stiffer surface on one side.

Doing What Really Counts

A lot of design effort and construction modification can go into an effort for improvement, but time and money may be spent on a part of the construction or form of performance modification that is not significant. Lowering the STC-measured transmission of airborne noise may be mostly a waste if the real culprit is structure-borne noise, flanking, leaks, or some other means of transmission. Or, raising the background noise level may be the most effective means for real improvement for the listeners, not modifications of the construction.

Be sure that you are working on the entire problem and on all the means for improvement, not performing a suboptimizing or misdirected exercise in futility.

6.5   STC RATING OF BARRIERS

The STC rating of a sound barrier is established by a standard test that measures the airborne sound transmission drop through the barrier at various frequencies. These performance data are displayed on a graph along with a standard noise reduction performance criterion curve. The standard noise reduction curve is then moved up and down on the graph until an acceptable relationship is determined between the performance data and the noise reduction reference curve (Figure 6.3). The effectiveness of the barrier at any specific frequency can then be judged from the relationship between the two curves.

The single value expressed as the STC is the decibel value of the criterion curve at a frequency of 500 Hz. While this is indeed in the middle of the high-sensitivity range for the human ear, it is the entire inferred relationship of the two curves that is understood from the rating.

In the end, the proof is in the real case: Does it work in real situations in some way related to the tested value? Theory is nice; science is good; engineering experience is a solid base; but if the wings fall off in the test flight, it will be time to go back to the designers before production starts.

For any barrier, there is some theoretical STC that can be determined on the basis of basic details of the construction of the barrier. What is it? A single sheet of glass? A stud partition with two layers of gypsum drywall on each side? In the test as well as in real installations, however, it is the entire construction process used for the barrier that counts. This means accounting for some other matters, such as the following:

Edges. A typical door or single partition has a top, bottom, and two side edges. These are potential sources for leaks, so stipulations for them must be part of the qualification of the barrier for a specific STC.

Holes. Glazing or ventilating louvers in doors may render them virtually sound transparent. Unsealed, back-to-back electrical switches or outlets can do the same for a relatively solid partition.

A particular door or wall construction may have a basic STC rating based on ordinary usage (in other words, nothing special done for sound attenuation) but have its value raised by various enhancing efforts. Doors may have sound-attenuating edge seals similar to weather-sealing for

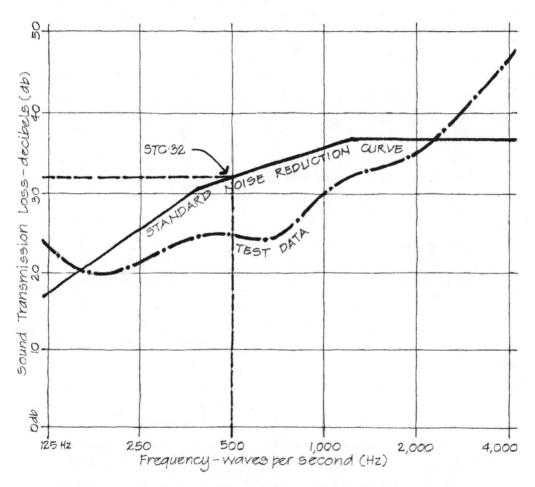

FIGURE 6.3 Determination of STC values. A standard test is performed on a barrier, consisting of measured sound transmission drops for various frequencies. The graph for these values is placed on a plot that also contains a standard noise reduction curve established for the class of the barrier. The noise reduction curve is moved up and down until a prescribed limit is obtained for the deviation of the test graph from the reference criteria curve. The STC value is then read as the decibel level at a frequency of 500 Hz on the graph. The single STC value thus implies more than the single frequency response of the barrier, since some relationship between the two graph lines is understood over the entire range of frequencies considered.

reduction of air loss. Partitions may be sealed at their edges to various degrees. Adjusted values for the STC of the barrier are the practical means for evaluating effectiveness of various means of enhancement.

Of course, the construction itself can be altered in many ways. The variations possible for a single stud frame partition with paneling materials on two sides is enormous (see Figure 6.4). A sampling is shown in the data displayed in the Appendix. Add all the other possibilities for construction of a wall from all available materials and products and the range is considerable. Still, for various reasons other than acoustic performance, a few very common forms of construction are widely used, the stud frame with paneling of drywall materials being the most common partition in most current construction.

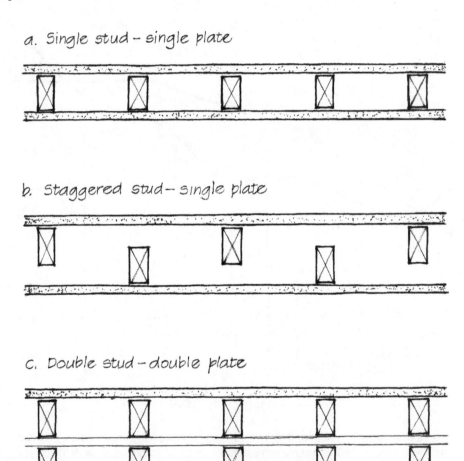

a. Single stud – single plate

b. Staggered stud – single plate

c. Double stud – double plate

FIGURE 6.4 Variation of basic stud construction. The attempt here is to isolate one surface from the other. This may be done by using two sets of studs on a single wide sill, as shown in the middle figure. Better yet, using two sills will further reduce the structural continuity. However, as always, attention must also be paid to leaks and various other problems or the modified construction may accomplish little of real significance.

For design purposes, STC values are commonly used in the following process.

1. A predicted, acceptable background noise level (in decibels) is determined for a room that receives airborne sound from a source in an adjacent space.
2. The predicted level of the noise source in the originating space is defined (in decibels).
3. An evaluation of the barrier in reducing airborne sound transmission is made—this is the STC in decibels. The resulting transmission is evaluated as acceptable if it drops the transmitted sound below the ambient background level in the room affected. If it is not acceptable, some modification of the barrier is considered.

We are dealing here with some fundamental relationships in terms of perceived loudness and possibly with some singular tasks in terms of sound privacy, audibility, or other specific requirements. Many factors can contribute to a single listening or communication task besides simple, single-frequency transmission effectiveness. However, if an affected space can generally be described and the originating source is generally qualified, a predictable range of effectiveness can probably be established for the sound-attenuating barriers for the affected space. On this basis, recommendations are made for the effective STC rating for barriers for common building situations. Table 6.1 gives representative data for this purpose.

Use of Table 6.1 for real design work is not recommended as the data base is quite old and was empirically derived. It is shown here mostly for the reader's understanding of the use of such data. Various building supervising agencies provide such data as design and construction recommendations or as actual requirements. However specific such data may be, they are always qualified by many approximations and subjective judgments, and their hair-splitting accuracy should always be questioned.

A further note of caution should be made regarding the real usefulness of exhaustive efforts to manipulate STC values. As discussed many times in this book, other sound behavior factors may really be more significant in any situation. Even for the sound barriers, the major problem might be impact noise (especially for floor/ceiling construction), and efforts to control that significantly may possibly also solve any STC-related problems, or some real combined design effort might be indicated. In other situations the major problem may be flanking or structure-borne sound from remote locations, adn the best efforts to improve STC ratings can be useless. Possible applications for use of STC ratings are discussed in the building case examples in Chapter 8.

TABLE 6.1   SIGNIFICANCE OF STC RATINGS OF BARRIERS[a]

Barrier STC	Effect on Hearing in Receiving Room	General Quality of Barrier	Possible Use
25			
	Normal conversation can be easily heard through the barrier.	Next to useless.	Separator for traffic or security; not for sound.
30			
	Loud sounds easily heard but normal conversation indistinct.	Fair; not much privacy.	Room divider where privacy and concentration are not important.
35			
	Loud sounds heard but not clear; normal speech very faint.	Fair to good.	For separation of relatively quiet rooms.
40			
	Loud sounds faintly heard; normal speech inaudible.	Good.	For separation of noisy from quiet spaces; marginally OK for party walls.
45			
	Most sounds not heard.	Very Good.	Generally acceptable for functional privacy.
50			
	Only very loud sounds faintly heard.	Excellent.	For sound studios; bedrooms next to noisy spaces.
55			

[a]Assuming a relatively quiet background in the receiving space, with NC-25 or so.

6.6   SUMMARY: DESIGN CONCERNS AND EFFORTS

General efforts to control airborne noises must usually be carried out within a combined design effort that includes other noise control factors. Nevertheless, it serves some useful purposes to consider the particular issue of airborne noise. To that end, the following is a checklist of considerations relating to the usual building design processes and common situations. For a broader view, see Sections 8.1 and 8.2.

1. Identify sensitive hearing/listening tasks and situations in terms of building occupancy and locations. Set specific goals for affected areas in terms of acceptable background noise levels and any special requirements.

2. Identify potential noise sources, critical sound paths, situations regarding adjacent quiet/noisy rooms, and elements of the construction likely to be critical for noise control.

3. Use ordinary architectural design options to achieve the best conditions for sound: planning; choice of basic construction; locations of doors, windows, and stairs; and site orientation.

4. Anticipate and define performance criteria for special sound needs, such as noise-emitting criteria for building equipment and its installation, and minimum performance requirements for elements of the construction (STC, IIC, absorption coefficients).

5. Do quick investigations of sound properties for all preliminary design options: reverberation times, STC, or ICC of proposed construction.

6. Evaluate special sound problems that indicate the need for acoustical expertise in design beyond your own experience and capabilities and obtain necessary consultation in early stages of the design work.

7

CONTROL OF IMPACT AND STRUCTURE-BORNE NOISE

In this chapter we treat the issue of structure-borne noise as a potential source of undesired sound for individual spaces in a building. The emphasis is on what can be done in the form of building planning and development of the construction to reduce the problems.

7.1 PLANNING AND CONSTRUCTION CONSIDERATIONS

In most situations three basic factors contribute to a structure-borne noise problem. Any planning or design efforts should start with a consideration of all three and some evaluation of which one or ones can most effectively be dealt with as design variables. The three basic factors are:

1. *Noise Source.* This is often a piece of building equipment (fan, toilet, slamming door, wall-mounted loudspeaker, etc.) but can be a piano, tap-dancing feet, balls bouncing off of walls, or other sources. Equipment may be selected for low noise emission, but many sources cannot be mitigated at the point of origin. Rubber-soled tap shoes or sponge rubber handballs just won't do.

2. *Sound Path.* A conveying structure that connects the source to some receiving point in the building; and to listeners at the receiving point. This is basically any continuous element of the

building construction; often, primarily the building structure, but it can be party walls, connecting doors, piping, ducts, or any element that has physical continuity from space to space.

3. *A Receiver.* A listener with a sound privacy or hearing task problem. Sound may also be received as airborne, which can be the *main* problem, so that a lot of effort to mitigate the structure-borne noise may not be well spent. Design should incorporate all the considerations.

Many of the techniques discussed in Chapter 6 for mitigation of airborne noise may also achieve improvement for structure-borne noise. This applies primarily to the reduction of direct transmission through separating barriers (walls and floors, mostly). However, there is a clear difference in the mechanisms of the two sound paths and in the responses of the construction, so that optimization for one type of sound reduction does not necessarily do the best job for others. It is desirable, therefore, to concentrate on the singular phenomenon of structure-borne noise to appreciate fully what is most relevant to its control.

7.2 SOURCES AND PATHS

Common sources of structure-borne noise are discussed in Chapter 5. If there are possibilities for reduction of the intensity level or other properties of the noise source itself, these should be pursued first. Acceptable criteria for building equipment should be given to the designers and specifiers of the equipment. If this necessitates use of special construction for installations, it should be understood early in the building design process.

Building Equipment

Permanently installed equipment will utilize many paths for structure-borne noise. This may be due to the form of its attachment, as mounted on walls, floors, ceilings, or rooftops. Equipment may be in an adjacent building with connecting below-grade construction (footings, tunnels, etc.). As noted previously, the "structure" achieving the sound path may be piping, ducts, other essentially nonstructural parts of the construction, or even the ground. Looking for all the possible paths is a real game of hide-and-seek.

Isolation of the Source or Mitigation of the Transmission

After doing everything possible to reduce the effects of the source itself, consideration should be given to basic *isolation* of the source. Noisy, vibrating equipment should in general not be rigidly mounted to the building structure. Non-conductive, cushioning materials or devices should be used to isolate the vibrating source from all of the continuous construction of the building.

A possibility in some cases is that of a sound-attenuating enclosure, effectively insulating the rest of the world from the noisy source. This may consist of modifications of the building construction itself or of the development of an entirely separate enclosure. The sound-separating enclosure may also certainly achieve reduction of airborne noise as well as structure-borne noise. This is often a highly effective method, but is also typically quite expensive, so other—less costly methods—should be fully explored first.

Sound-attenuating enclosures can utilize most of the criteria and techniques developed for sound control by the building construction in general. However, since they relate to a very specific source, they can be customized to a higher degree, and their design should indeed concentrate on measures most effective for the particular source and potential affected listeners.

Once possibilities for mitigating the source itself have been exhausted, efforts may be made to decouple or isolate the source from potential structural paths. Vibration and sound-attenuating mountings, floating slabs, and other techniques may serve to isolate the source from the path sufficiently to eliminate the need for further consideration for this path form. With a single source and many potential disturbed listeners, this is a way to avoid other extensive, costly modifications of the basic building construction.

When all of the preceding is not feasible or is ineffective, attention must be given to the basic structural paths and their potential for modification. In addition to high cost, the real possibility of achieving modifications that work may rely heavily on very thorough and realistic inspections during the construction work. Extra measures and out-of-the-ordinary details for ordinary construction can be disturbing or confusing for workers, and shortcuts can render the results ineffective. The same precautions regarding modifications for reduction of leaks and flanking for airborne noise apply here—this is an *extra* effort for the builders.

Transmission Capacity of the Construction

Basic forms of construction vary in their degree of potential for structure-borne noise and in the potentially for mitigating modifications. Density of materials and the degree of continuity of the construction are major factors. Thus the potential is naturally higher for structures of steel, concrete, and masonry than it is for structures of wood, plastic, or various synthetic composites. Natural properties of the construction should be carefully evaluated in this regard before any expensive modifications are considered. Properties are not the same for all types of sound-source or listening situations.

Modification of the basic building construction may also have to deal with more than one sound source and with many different listening situations. It makes it additionally complicated when consideration for all the other performance requirements besides sound are added to the design decisions. This is quite often the real situation for many buildings, which works to make modifications of the basic construction the *last* resort instead of the *first* consideration for mitigation of structure-borne noise.

7.3 IMPACT NOISE

Impact noise is a form of structure-borne noise, typically created by something striking a part of the building, usually a floor or wall. Common examples are slamming doors, dropped objects, people running, athletic events involving flying objects (handballs, basketballs, bowling balls, hockey pucks), and moving vehicles hitting bumps. The impact can produce a combination of airborne sound, structure-borne sound, and actual physical sensation of the impact force itself, even if you cannot hear it.

As in other situations, control of the source is the best solution, and any possible efforts in this regard should be pursued first. Don't share the wall of the handball court with the library. Don't put apartments over the bowling alley.

When planning options are exhausted, do all the usual things possible with the affected intervening construction. If airborne and ordinary structure-borne factors are involved, the usual solutions are still available. However, a characteristic of this source is usually its short-duration rather than enduring nature. This is significantly different from a continuous fan noise or a blaring TV set. It may be repeated—as in a bouncing basketball or running feet—but the single individual impact is a sharp sound of short duration and a single physical jolt if felt directly.

For use in evaluation of floors and walls as both separating construction and the receiving surface for impacts, a standard rating system has been established called the *impact insulation class* (IIC). This is a single-figure measurement rating of the estimated effectiveness of the separating construction for reduction of impact. It is used primarily for relative comparisons of the effectiveness of various different forms of construction and of various techniques for attenuation of the barrier. Standard tests involving a dropped object are used to establish IIC values.

Figure 7.1 shows the situation of an object dropped on a floor and the transmission of the noise to an affected space below. The two general means for attenuation are to reduce the sound effect by cushioning or isolating it (Figure 7.1A and B) or by insulating the affected area with a resilient-supported ceiling or other means (Figure 7.1C and D).

Anything remotely effective in mitigating impact noises will probably result in significant improvements for all other noise problems, both airborne and structure-borne. Use of carpeting and lightweight concrete fill on top of wood floor structures is now quite common for apartments, hotels, and office buildings, its effectiveness in the attenuation of impact noises being a major reason. Some specific conditions relating to typical occupancies and forms of construction are discussed in Chapter 8.

7.4   STRATEGIES FOR CONTROL

First consideration should be given to the possibilities for the *elimination* of structure-borne noise sources. If total elimination is not possible, then some specific criteria should be established for the *mitigation* of the source. If it truly has a potential for being disturbing, then to what degree can the source itself be reduced in impact on listeners? These efforts should precede any design work for modifications of the construction.

Considerations for techniques for design of modifications for control of structure-borne noise should begin with an analysis of the potentially

A. CUSHION IMPACT   B. FLOAT FLOOR   C. SUSPEND CEILING   D. SOUND ABSORBER
                                                                        IN CAVITY

FIGURE 7.1   Impact noise. The major, common concern for impact is the effect of objects dropped on or otherwise striking floor surfaces. For construction considerations, this involves the transmission of a structure-borne sound through the floor/ceiling system, emerging as an airborne sound in the lower space. Treatments typically involve cushioning of the floor (carpet, etc.), isolation of the ceiling (suspending versus direct attachment), or some modification of the basic floor structure (thicker concrete, concrete fill added to a wood deck, etc.). An additional possibility is the so-called *floated floor*, produced by using a layer of sound-isolating material in the construction, usually immediately above the structural deck. For the best solution, of course, all of these tricks may be used together. From *A Guide to Airborne, Impact, and Structureborne Noise Control in Multifamily Dwellings* (Ref. 2).

disturbed listeners. Incoming noise for them may simply be a general annoyance, may actually interfere with or completely prevent some hearing task, or may be a source of real hearing injury in extreme cases. This should be a basic source for some specific criteria for noise reduction on a performance requirement basis, which should precede any design efforts in response to the matters discussed in the preceding section.

Essential concerns for the listeners are their listening or communication tasks, the background noise level in the space they occupy, and the particular form of incoming noise (intensity level, frequency, endurance over time, etc.). In other words, what is it in particular about the incoming noise that is disturbing and needs mitigation? Is it, in fact, quite possible that modification of the listening situation might sufficiently reduce the impact of the incoming noise so as to make it possible to endure or ignore it? Maybe the addition of some white noise to raise the level of the background noise and mask the incoming noise is the easiest and most effective technique, even though it is not much within the control of the building designers.

An essential point to be made here is that some real criteria are needed before any design modifications are undertaken. Is the fan really too noisy, or is it within a tolerable limit in decibel level? Do not buy another, maybe less energy-efficient, fan or design expensive mountings or enclosures if they are not really needed.

A second major point is to be sure that efforts go first to the most effective and most easily achieved means of design modification. Is it reduction at the source, isolation of the source, decoupling from the structure, modification of the structure, insulation of the listener, or modification of the listening experience?

Finally, a third point is to be sure that concentration on structure-borne sound is not an exercise in suboptimization while other factors are really more critical. Is it really primarily an airborne sound problem? Extensive modification of the structure will not make up for an open window, flanking through ducts, or a leaky door or electrical outlet. Try to find the real culprit.

Various situations for potential structure-borne sound problems are discussed in Chapter 8, together with possible means for their mitigation through design.

7.5 ARCHITECTURAL AND STRUCTURAL PROBLEMS

Sound-behavior properties of the building construction affect all types of sound control problems. However, they can be somewhat more problematic as they relate to impact and structure-borne sound. In both cases the construction itself can become a sound source, broadcasting sound into the affected spaces.

Many long-standing construction practices and favorite forms of construction have really bad potential for sound problems. The extensive use of light wood framing in the United States has produced a lot of truly sound-transparent buildings. This affects transmission of airborne noises (low natural STC values) but can also contribute to impact problems and other structure-borne problems.

The typical, minimal floor/ceiling construction, as shown in Figure 7.2*a*, produces a structure that very efficiently transmits all structure-borne noises unless some attenuating details are added. All the techniques shown in Figure 7.1 for a concrete slab can also be used here, but one simple, common response is as shown in Figure 7.2*b*, with the addition of carpeting, a concrete fill, a separating/isolating layer between the finish floor and the structure, and resilient attachment for the drywall ceiling. More could be done actually, but these measures are usually sufficient in their combination for separation of the levels in a motel, apartment building, or small office building. Significant improvements are made in both STC and IIC values.

A special problem with any structure, not apparent in acoustic measurements, is the possibility for transmission or broadcast through the structure of dynamic loadings in a directly sensed manner. If someone slams a door really hard in a light frame building, it may quite likely be "felt" throughout the building, even if sound conditioning substantially reduces the audibility or apparent loudness for the ear. If you cannot hear it at all, you may still know that something bumped the building hard. Nothing short of a really heavy, massive building structure will reduce the direct sensation.

Solid, continuous structures have their own problems, however. For modifications of the floor with a separating layer, as shown in Figures 7.1 and 7.2, an effectiveness may be achieved in a vertical transmission as shown, but if the floating floor is not separated at its edges from the walls, the game may be lost. In this case the solid, continuous nature of the floor's supporting structure becomes a means for coupling of the floor and supported walls—and of the floor to that under the rooms next door.

FIGURE 7.2   Sound separation with wood-framed floors. The typical construction (a) with wood joists, a plywood deck, a hard-finished surface with wood flooring or thin tile over a wood fiber underlay, and a drywall ceiling attached to the underside of the joists has generally poor performance for both STC and IIC values. Anything will help, but the more the better. The modification shown in (b) has four elements: (1) a carpet and pad for impact reduction; (2) a concrete fill for improved structural stiffness and mass and additional insulative value; (3) a sound-separating underlay on top of the deck and under the concrete fill; and (4) resilient furring to decouple the ceiling drywall surface. The net effect of these modifications will be substantial improvements in both STC and IIC values. With a suspended ceiling it may be possible to use resilient spring isolators for suspension (c), which may reduce the necessity for some of the measures used with the floor assemblage if the main problem is structure-borne noise.

a. Standard Floor-Ceiling Construction:
  • HIGH PROBABILITY OF STRUCTUREBORNE NOISE TRANSMISSION

Hardwood T·G flooring
Plywood subfloor

Joists

Gypsum board ceiling

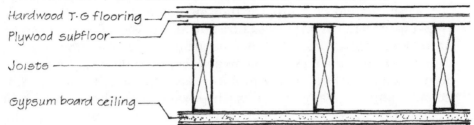

b. Composite Floor-Ceiling Assembly with structural separation and resiliency
  • LOW PROBABILITY OF STRUCTUREBORNE NOISE TRANSMISSION

Carpet on resilient pad
Concrete fill
Sound absorbing mat
Plywood subfloor

Joists

Resilient channel
Gypsum board ceiling

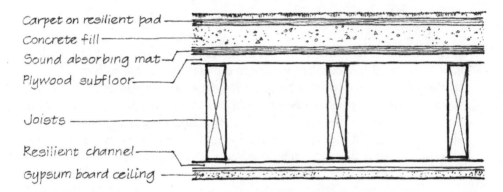

c. Composite Floor-Ceiling Assembly - structural isolation and resiliency
  • LOW PROBABILITY OF STRUCTUREBORNE NOISE TRANSMISSION

Carpet on resilient pad
Plywood subfloor

Joists

Resilient·spring isolators

Gypsum panels-tiles

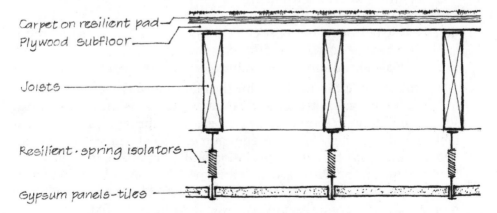

A sturdy, solid structure may mitigate the direct sensation but will still very efficiently and rapidly carry the structure-borne noise a long distance, transmitting it to everything firmly attached to it along the way.

Chasing air leaks for airborne transmission by leaks and flanking is one kind of search; trying to visualize how and to where the structure can carry sound, vibrations, and general dynamic impacts is another.

Some examples of these problems and their relations to general architectural and structural design problems are presented in Chapter 8. If sound control is really critical, such problems may be dealt with in various ways. However, as is often the case, other criteria may prevail: fire safety, structural efficiency, thermal properties, or dollar cost of the construction frequently take higher priority.

7.6 SUMMARY: DESIGN CONCERNS AND EFFORTS

General efforts to control impact and structure-borne noises ought to be carried out within a combined design effort that includes other noise control factors as well as problems of direct physical vibrations. Nevertheless, it serves some useful purposes to consider the particular issues of impact and structure-borne noise. To that end, the following is a checklist of considerations relating to the usual building design processes and common situations. For a broader view, see Sections 8.1 and 8.2.

1. Identify and evaluate sensitive listening and communication tasks in terms of building occupancy and locations. Set specific goals for listeners and areas affected in terms of acceptable background noise levels and any special requirements.

2. Identify and evaluate potential noise sources, critical sound paths, situations of adjacent quiet/noisy rooms, and elements of the construction likely to be critical for noise control. For impact, the particular problem of floor noises carried to affected spaces below should be studied. Provide goals for minimum IIC values for floor construction.

3. Make every effort to determine the planning and equipment needs for the plumbing, electrical, and HVAC systems, as these are typical sources for structure-borne noise and general vibration problems. Establish limiting values for noise emission of critical items of equipment and specifications for sound insulation and other attenuation methods for ducts and piping. Provide details and specifications for elimination of sound leaks through penetrations of the wall and floor construction by piping, electrical conduits, outlets, switches, plumbing fixtures, and so on.

4. Use common architectural design alternatives to achieve the best conditions for sound: planning, choice of basic construction, locations of noisy equipment, and so on.

5. Anticipate and provide data for special sound needs of spaces with urgent listening tasks or high levels of sound privacy.

8

CASE STUDIES: BUILDING DESIGN SITUATIONS

The purpose of this chapter is to present a number of examples of building uses, building forms, construction usages, and site situations, and to illustrate possibilities for consideration of sound control for each example. The presentations here are meant to complement the materials in preceding chapters. Basic issues and relationships are dealt with more extensively in those chapters, and that material should be used as a resource for the more detailed information on individual situations shown in these examples.

However, designers must ordinarily face the problem of the entire construction process, even though the actual design may be worked out by concentrating on one problem at a time. Here the presentation begins with consideration of the building's general form and construction system, followed by presentation of some of the primary increments of the construction with all the significant parts displayed. The discussion then proceeds to consideration of major service systems, with some emphasis on factors that significantly affect the development of sound controls for various possible design goals.

The building designs presented in this chapter are not meant as illustrations of superior architecture. The interest here is directed mostly to setting up reasonably realistic situations that cover a range of circumstances with regard to construction design. It is not the intention to present boring, ugly buildings, but the use of a limited number of examples to display a broad range of situations is the dominant concern.

An attempt has been made to show construction usage and the form of details that are reasonably correct. This is, however, a matter for much individual judgment and is often tempered by time and location. There are not many situations in which only one way is correct and all others are unequivocally wrong.

Reasonably correct alternatives are often possible, and the particular circumstances for an individual building can make a specific choice better on different occasions. Differences in climate, building codes, local markets, building experience, or community values can produce a way of doing things that is preferred. Over time, changes in any of those areas of influence will produce variety and hopefully some evolution toward a better way of doing things.

The concentration in this book is on sound control and its relations to the general building planning and development of the construction. General form and construction details of the buildings are presented here only to the extent necessary to understand the basic development of the construction, with emphasis on those parts that especially relate to sound control issues.

The approach to design for sound control should begin with some general consideration for sound problems as they relate to typical building construction and use. In Section 8.1 we present some general concerns and a checklist of basic considerations. These have been presented as summaries at the ends of the preceding chapters, relating to the limited topics of the individual chapters. The summary here is made to include the overall approach to design for improved sound conditions.

In Section 8.2 we continue this general approach by presenting some of the most common problem situations that occur with many different occupancies and uses. Design for specific occupancies typically means solving many of these common problems first and then giving any necessary additional attention to the special problems that may occur.

In the remainder of the sections in this chapter we present discussions relating to common occupancy situations and building uses. For any individual building design, a systematic approach to design for sound control should begin with the general concerns described in Section 8.1, then consider the possibilities for problems of the generic type described in Section 8.2, and finally, proceed to any special problems relating to the specific building use or circumstances.

8.1 GENERAL BUILDING SOUND PROBLEMS

A broad approach to design for sound control should begin with general consideration for what typical situations or inherent problems there might be in any building. The common considerations include the following.

Need for Specific Interior Conditions

Just about any building use entails the need for some type of sound condition, in terms of sound privacy or a specific listening task. A first step in any design for sound control is the identification of goals for individual building spaces and the establishment of specific performance objectives for those spaces. This is the fundamental source for any data for use in evaluating performance of designed elements of the building.

Identification may be established on a broad basis by a general occupancy: housing, office, assembly, and so on. Individual spaces may be identified more specifically in terms that relate to particular sound privacy needs or listening tasks: bedroom, private office, study room, recording studio, and so on.

Identification of Offensive Noise Sources

Noise is unwanted sound, causing a lack of privacy or actually interfering with a listening task, such as hearing a lecture. Once a desired interior condition has been defined, all possible sources for disturbance of that condition should be investigated. For actual design work, the complete investigation must include consideration of the sound transmission pathways and their specific relationships to building planning and construction.

If the space affected has an established ideal background noise level, some useful data may be determined for the attenuation performance of the enclosure construction (walls, floors) or other elements of the sound pathways (doors, ducts).

More general identifications may establish goals for spatial planning, isolation mountings, or other devices to mitigate the sound source. For equipment, some target values may be established for sound-emitting properties (fan noise, etc.).

Inherent Problems with the Building Construction

If the use of a particular form of construction is anticipated, the usual limitations and effectiveness of that construction with regard to sound performance should be considered in early design work. It is not reasonable to set certain goals if the basic construction cannot feasibly be modified to produce the necessary attenuation of sound transmissions. Settle for what is reasonably attainable, or consider changing the basic construction if sound control is of really high priority.

Inherent Problems with the Building Site

Is it an urban site with many other buildings and activities close by? Is it an isolated site in the country? Is it next door to a factory? Is it near an airport? Money spent on interior sound attenuation may be wasted if incoming sounds from external sources are overwhelming. Attenuation of the building's exterior skin may be a principal necessity.

Inherent Problems with the Building Planning

Are there basic problem situations for sound that are essentially unavoidable because of required planning considerations? How much separation can you give to separate rooms in a motel, to separate apartments in a high-rise apartment building, to separate classrooms in a school, or to separate offices in a large office building? Large fans and air-cooling equipment must be put *somewhere*; it simply may not be possible to isolate them spatially from all the occupied building spaces.

Look for what must be expected for various occupancies in terms of planning that is likely to present problems for sound control.

Rate the Likely Importance of Sound Problems

This means determining the predominant or major problems in any situation. Modifications for subtle adjustments of room acoustics may be useless if incoming noise is overwhelming. Attack the big problems first and work down to the finer adjustments.

Invest Wisely

If the budget is limited (isn't it always?), spend it for the most effective efforts in terms of benefit/cost payoff. Where many different adjustments may contribute to the mitigation of a particular problem, some will be more expensive than others. Is their cost directly related to their effectiveness, or may some simple, inexpensive alterations be most effective?

Consider Special Sound Problems

Are you planning to put bedrooms over a bowling alley? A private office next to a metal shop? A lecture hall under a gymnasium? Or are you designing a theater, a sound recording studio, or other very special occupancy regarding sound control? These situations go well beyond simple means for basic sound control. Don't kid yourself, you need real help from highly experienced acoustic specialists.

8.2 TYPICAL BUILDING SOUND SITUATIONS

For any building there are various probable situations that occur repeatedly. Before special problems relating to a particular building use are considered, it is wise to look for these generic problems. The following are classic cases of sound control problems that occur in many buildings.

Bad Room for Its Purpose

Any individual room may be configured, constructed, or generally situated to respond badly to internal sound conditions regarding listening tasks. Once a room usage is identified and any sound privacy or listening tasks are identified, some evaluation should be made of the features that create a good sound condition—and if they are not present will probably create a bad sound condition. This may involve room shape, dimensions, proportions of dimensions (length to width, etc.), specially formed surfaces (pleated, porous, etc.), general surfacing materials (regarding absorption), locations of doors or windows, and so on.

Special Sound Problems

A room or space may have extra requirements or a special problem, including special usages such as lecture rooms, theaters, or recording studios. Some extreme cases of various situations are described below. Such cases produce requirements that are likely to demand something beyond the usual planning and construction, and real goals and quantified design criteria should be established in very early stages of the building design work.

These spaces should be favored in all the ways possible in terms of basic planning relating to location with respect to noisy spaces or equipment, basic type of room-enclosing construction, isolation from structure-borne noise paths, and so on. Special construction will probably still be necessary, but it shouldn't have to overcome a whole list of ordinary, avoidable problems first.

Quiet Room/Noisy Room Side by Side

Any two rooms with a shared wall have the potential for a sound transmission problem through the separating barrier. A survey should be made of any planning options to see what is next to what in terms of noise, privacy, and listening task relationships. Unavoidable adjacent placements may present the need for attenuation of the separating walls, as well as study for problems of leaks, flanking, impact, or structure-borne sounds.

The first choice will always be for better planning to eliminate the adjacency, but if this is not possible, acoustic design must be anticipated for good sound control results. The feasibility of the basic wall construction for enhanced sound attenuation should be considered in early design decisions.

Quiet Room/Noisy Room Above and Below

With the noise source below, the main problem will be the STC rating of the floor/ceiling construction, plus any possible leaks or flanking. If the noisy space is above, it may involve all the possibilities for airborne, structure-borne, and impact noises, requiring consideration for STC, IIC, isolation, insulation, and whatever can be done.

If the sound flow is in one direction, it may be best to insulate the space affected. If the noise source is affecting many other spaces, it may be possible to isolate the noisy space by a total attenuating enclosure. If a major problem is impact noise, the use of a floating floor with a sound-isolating layer in the floor construction and buffered edges at all walls may protect the rest of the structure and the space immediately below.

Noise-Broadcasting Centers

Large fans, pumps, and heavy elements of cooling systems may be isolated in individual locations or grouped in really noisy bunches in a rooftop, basement, or other location. These may be sources for both airborne and structure-borne noise and even major, physically sensible vibrations. Resilient mountings and possibly sound-attenuating enclosures may be necessary. But all possible options for isolation by planning should be explored first.

Gathering places for meetings, recreation, or entertainment in buildings or complexes with otherwise relatively quiet areas (office buildings, apartments, schools, libraries, hospitals, etc.) should also preferably be separated by distance first, then by any necessary attenuating construction.

Loud TV sets or stereo systems are probably the least controllable and most common offending sources. Successful solutions begin with some architectural planning and design considerations, but individual users can contribute a lot in sheer volume or in placement of equipment. Wall-mounted speakers firmly bolted to the structure are hard to fight.

Parking Facilities

Outdoor parking lots next to buildings or indoor parking anywhere create a source for various sounds. Starting of cars, revving of engines, slamming of doors and trunks, and some squealing of tires are all unavoidable. Honking, jackrabbit takeoffs, and car alarms are not necessary but inevitable. Like boom-boxes, this is a fact of modern life that is difficult to deal with.

Really Tough Sound Problems

The more you know about them, the more you may be able to anticipate some really tough sound problems. If real expertise is required, an experienced acoustic consultant should be used, and the earlier the better. If the expert is called in only after the occupants are in the building, the most expensive solution possible is likely to be the result.

8.3   HOUSING

The general case of housing presents an array of situations, the two basic variants being single-family houses and multiple-family housing. The single, freestanding house is a fading dream for most families but still a lucrative market for building designers, especially the small office that must, for practical reasons often work without very many specialty consultants. For that reason we will first consider this anachronistic example.

Building 1 in Figure 8.1 is a building of modest proportions, not impressive to architectural critics but a castle by world housing standards. The form of house shown here is a typical suburban split-level, but many details are really reminiscent of the basic Cape Cod cottage.

Figures 8.2 and 8.3 show the details for the general building construction. As shown here, the light wood-frame construction system provides considerable hollow, interstitial space which can be used extensively for installation of out-of-view piping and wiring and some built-in elements of the various service systems. Some elements of the latter type that are routinely accommodated in this fashion are power outlets, light switches, wall and ceiling HVAC registers, and some recessed ceiling light fixtures. It is very important to understand the form of the various service elements, as they present some possible noise sources and typically a lot of potential for sound leaks, flanking, and crosstalk.

There are two situations shown in the construction details, however, where burying of service elements is somewhat of a problem. Details C, D, and F show the concrete slab floor and foundations. These solid concrete elements offer less accommodation to burying of elements, although some wiring is occasionally so treated as well as small items such as power outlets.

Another situation of this type is shown in detail E2 in Figure 8.3. With the plank roof deck, any elements for services at the ceiling must probably be surface mounted or suspended, whereas the use of the light wood construction shown in detail E1 would permit relatively easy concealing of any wiring, recessed lights, or even small ducts.

Figure 8.4 shows the general scheme for development of an all-air HVAC system for building 1. There are several possible variations on this

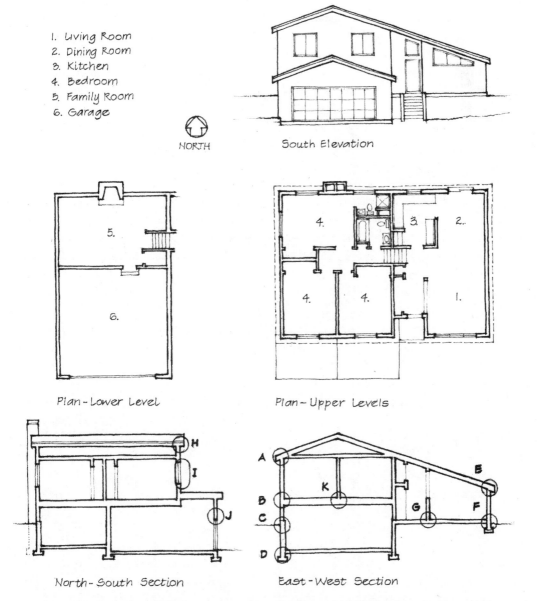

1. Living Room
2. Dining Room
3. Kitchen
4. Bedroom
5. Family Room
6. Garage

NORTH

South Elevation

Plan – Lower Level

Plan – Upper Levels

North – South Section

East – West Section

FIGURE 8.1 Single-family house, an icon of the American Dream. Not quite a castle, but about as out of reach as one to the majority of the population. Cost of land and infrastructure makes for close packing of houses in new developments, somewhat blurring the line between this and multifamily housing. Thus many of the problems visualized for apartments in Figure 5.1 also apply here. Widespread use of light wood-frame construction creates a starting point with a quite sound-transparent structure for development of any sound privacy. Low-density materials and zillions of leaks are hard to overcome. Separation of sound-interactive spaces by planning and suppression or decoupling of noise sources are the principal means for improvement for sound control.

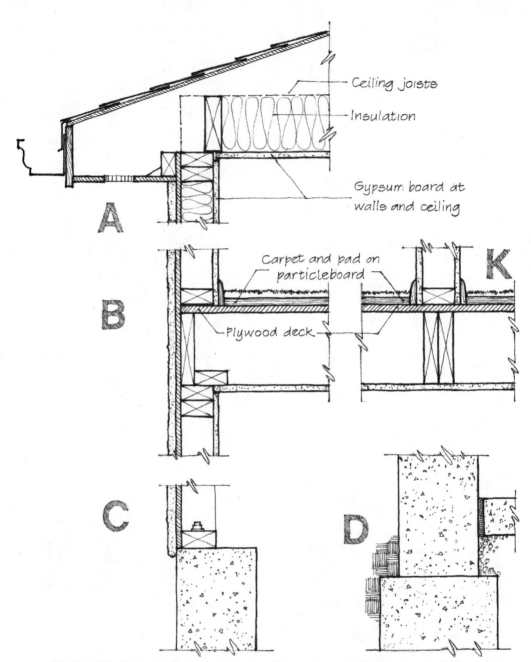

FIGURE 8.2 Construction details for the light wood frame. Appearance is infinitely modifiable, but the basic structure is typically altered very little for most houses. Hollow walls and floors provide for a lot of concealed wiring and piping, which results in a lot of potential leaks through the already not so good barriers. Without blocking, horizontal channels can be formed by the parallel floor joists. Insulation, duplicate framing, extra caution for edge and joint sealing, seals for wall fixtures, and stiffer or denser surfacing can improve sound separation (higher STC), but adjacent rooms are going to interact to a considerable degree in the best of situations. Separate floors can be treated like separate apartments with improvement of the floor/ceiling construction (see Figure 7.2); carpeting and a concrete fill will accomplish a lot. Exterior walls will also be transparent for outdoor sounds, especially through any operable windows. It is not a totally lost cause, but any design goals should be realistic.

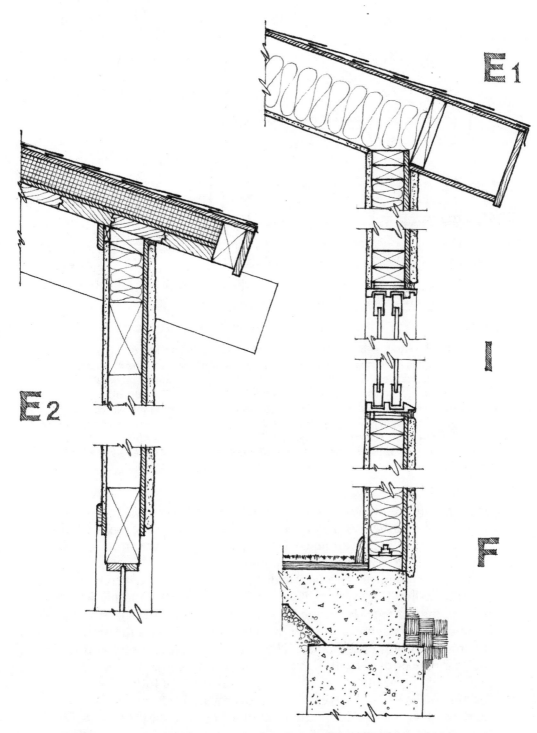

FIGURE 8.3 Roof construction without an attic space. This provides an upper reflecting surface that can aim sounds where they might not be wanted. Ordinary drywall, hard plaster, or an exposed plank deck will not absorb much, so the geometry should be studied to see where this major reflector is sending sound.

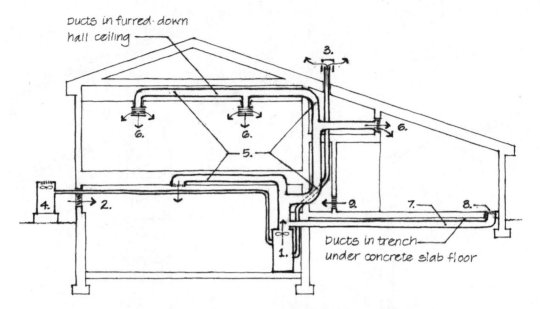

Ducts in furred-down hall ceiling

Ducts in trench under concrete slab floor

FIGURE 8.4 HVAC system. Other than flushing toilets, slamming doors, and kitchen appliances, this is the major noise source, providing both airborne and structure-borne noises. Air ducts are efficient broadcast channels and can help with crosstalk between separate rooms, even on different sides or floors of the house. Rooftop, attic, or outdoor units will also produce noise for the neighborhood. Attenuating the enclosure of the sources (fans, mostly), selecting equipment that is low in emitted noise, and decoupling everything from the structure may accomplish improvements worth pursuing. Dealing with the ducts is trickier, and anything effective is probably expensive in terms of extra construction.

system, with certain forms more appropriate for particular climatic conditions. Shown here is a system that favors air conditioning (cooling) through use of high-wall registers, a system more appropriate for warm climates where heating is not a major concern.

In cooler climates, especially if air conditioning is not developed by the central air-handling system, it would probably be better to use a system with perimeter registers in the floor. For the construction, this would be relatively easily achieved within the light wood frame for the upper-level bedroom portion of the house. However, the floor registers and feeder ducts for the portions with slab floors would be somewhat more difficult. This might favor the use of crawl space construction for the living room portion of the house. Use of the crawl space would also make it somewhat easier to assure warm floors and a better response to the problems of edge heat loss at the ground level.

Separately developed—although with some similar construction details—are the ventilation exhaust systems for the bathrooms and kitchen. Use of dropped ceilings in these areas greatly simplifies these installations.

Figure 8.5 shows the general nature of the plumbing systems for water supply and waste. Again, the light wood frame is reasonably accommodating for these installations. In fact, it is almost too easy to hack up the

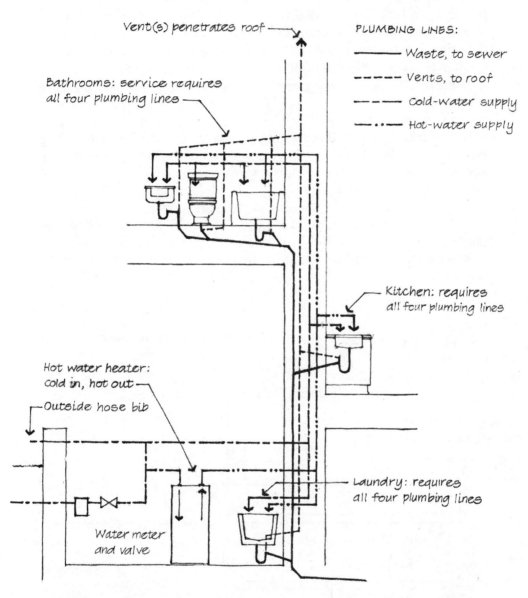

FIGURE 8.5 Plumbing: piping and fixtures served. Start with the piping—it can vibrate and it can gurgle. Insulate it, attenuate any enclosure, keep it far away from affected areas, and decouple it from the structure. Seal any penetrations through the construction of sound barriers for piping and wall-hung or wall-recessed fixtures. Buy a quieter toilet. Use metal, not plastic, drain piping. Do what you can to isolate showers and toilets. Better than all of this is to use planning to separate affected areas; just don't put the toilet or shower over or next to a space where you don't want to hear it.

light wood frame, resulting in some serious losses of the structural frame in some cases. Generally, the structure has considerable redundancy and load sharing by the closely spaced members, but careful inspection should be made to assure the structural integrity of the frame after the plumbers and electricians get through with it. This is important for structural reasons but is also a major area of concern for sound control. Leaks for airborne sound and contacts for structure-borne sound can be created extensively during the installation of these service systems.

Some details for the basic electrical power system are shown in Figure 8.6. Figure 8.7 shows some details for lighting elements that are built into the construction. Wiring for lighting is integrated with that for the general power distribution, while the wiring for low-voltage systems (including phones and cable TV) is separately, and somewhat more casually, developed in the construction. Figure 8.8 shows some details for the various low-voltage electrical systems.

Altogether, there is a lot of wiring in the average, simple residence, and the popularity of the light wood frame stems significantly from its abundant interstitial spaces which comfortably accommodates this wiring, as well as the many built-in electrical components and fixtures served by the

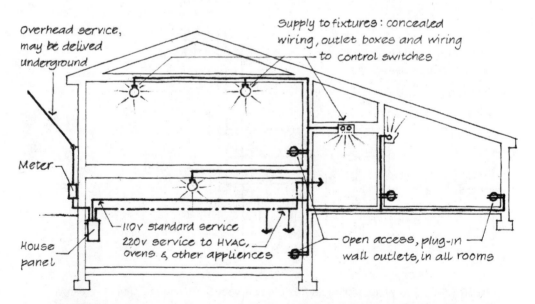

FIGURE 8.6 Electric power and lighting. Wiring in conduits becomes much like piping—carrying sounds and penetrating the construction. Wall outlets, switches, and mounted or recessed lighting will penetrate barriers endlessly. If you spend money for an enhanced sound barrier (wall or floor), make sure that all the penetrations get extra attention for sealing of leaks. Use quiet switches—a snapped switch will broadcast as structure-borne noise through the conduits and the basic construction.

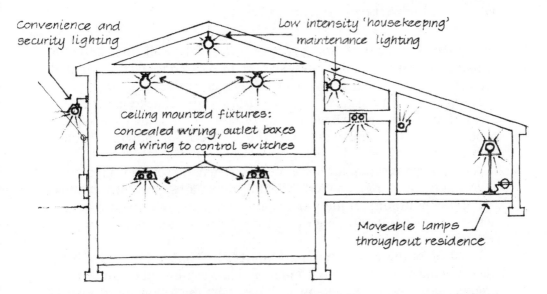

Convenience and security lighting

Low intensity 'housekeeping' maintenance lighting

Ceiling mounted fixtures: concealed wiring, outlet boxes and wiring to control switches

Moveable lamps throughout residence

FIGURE 8.7 Lighting. Hard-wired fixtures (installed in the construction) will make penetrations of the barriers. Some forms of lighting (fluorescent, etc.) will produce noise. A special problem is the coordinated development of surfaces that reflect both light and sound.

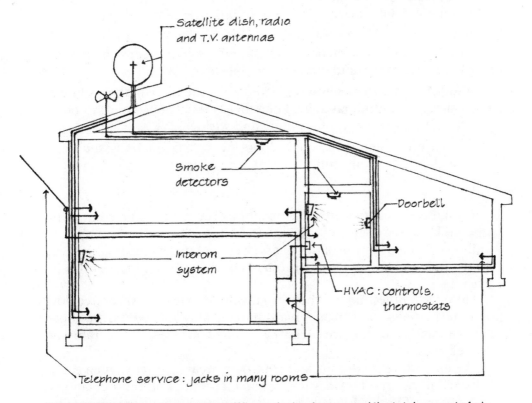

Satellite dish, radio and T.V. antennas

Smoke detectors

Doorbell

Interom system

HVAC: controls, thermostats

Telephone service: jacks in many rooms

FIGURE 8.8 Other wired services. We are device-happy, and the total amount of wiring, both installed and draped around, is staggering in the average house. Be sure to consider all you know of these sources for penetration of the sound barriers.

wiring systems. The total number of punctures of the wall, floor, and ceiling construction required for these systems in enormous and the potential for airborne sound leaks is correspondingly extensive.

Design considerations for sound control should relate to specific concerns of the occupants. The following discussions assume some typical concerns that will surely vary in level of concern for individual house owners.

A first concern is that for noise sources. A general source is that of the HVAC and plumbing elements. Whistling ducts, air supply fans, exhaust fans, air-conditioning chillers and heat exchangers, toilets, showers, garbage disposals, and gurgling drain piping are all common sources of objectionable noises.

Isolation of these potential noise sources by zoned planning may be ideal, but the need for a compact plan and accessibility of facilities often predominates. What remains in such cases are the following efforts:

Reduction of the noise source by oversizing piping and ducts, choice of low sound-emitting equipment, and any other means possible

Use of isolation mountings and attachments for elements with vibration potential, especially large fans and air-conditioning units

Enhancements of the construction for especially critical elements, such as walls between bedrooms, and floor/ceiling construction between bedrooms and other, noisier places

Careful attention to potential objectionable leaks and flanking sources caused by continuous ducts, holes for electrical outlets and switches, and chases and holes for piping and wiring

Possible use of sound-enhanced doors for special situations, such as a mechanical room, toilets, or places desiring a high degree of privacy

Beyond noise control are concerns for privacy and sound comfort in general. The large open entry/living room/dining/kitchen area may generally be "quieted" by use of thick carpet, an "acoustical" ceiling, draperies at windows, and any wall treatments to reduce sound reflections in general.

The open connecting stair between the three levels allows for free flow of sound between these areas. If planning can allow for doors at the upper and middle levels, the areas can be sound-separated considerably as desired at times.

The upper-level, bedroom, and bathroom areas are pretty much going to have limited sound privacy for individual rooms. Loud conversations, high-volume TVs, flushing toilets, and jumping on floors are going to be shared by all the occupants. The tight planning and the light wood frame construction make any efforts for serious sound conditioning pretty futile. Family compatibility and love are going to be the main sources for happiness in terms of sound conditions.

Other than the working of doors into the level-separating stairs, the other investment worth considering is some attenuation of the floor/ceiling construction to reduce transmission of noise from the garage and family room to the bedrooms above.

All of the concerns and situations just described for the single-family house have the potential for occurrence in individual units of multiple-family buildings. However, the principal sound problem for multiple-family housing is typically that of acoustic separation between individual housing units. Having discussed most of the problems within a unit, we consider this issue primarily for the multiple-unit housing structure.

Multiple units are typically separated by common walls or by floor/ceiling construction. For interception of both airborne and structure-borne sounds, the basic construction for these elements may be enhanced to various degrees by the means discussed in Chapters 6 and 7. Careful attention must also be given, however, to all the possibilities for leaks, flanking, crosstalk, and general structure-borne sounds that can be carried through common, continuous elements of the construction and the service systems.

Of course, all possibilities should be exhausted first for planning for sound separation. Placing one apartment's bathroom next to a common wall with another apartment's bedroom on the other side of the wall is asking for the most trouble possible. Placing operable windows for separate apartments only a few feet apart on a single wall is guaranteeing an unavoidable flanking problem. Just a little study of the plans should reveal these and other basic problems. If the study is done in time, the entire sound control effort will be made more effective and much easier to achieve.

Real sound control for noise reduction and privacy comes with a price tag here, and the general economic level of the occupants is likely to be a concern for design goals. There is a lot of distance to go beyond the basic requirements of current housing design standards.

Several of the illustrations, some of the data, and some discussions presented in this book are taken from a dated but still major reference produced by the FHA (Federal Housing Association) in the late 1960s (Ref. 2). This publication deals specifically with the problems of large apartment buildings, but the situations treated have many parallels in other occupancy situations, most notably motels, hotels, and dormitories, but also any place where many people occupy separate spaces tightly packed into a single structure.

8.4   SCHOOLS

Educational facilities range in level from preschool to universities and may consist of a single building or a whole community. Although all the usual problems can occur in terms of noisy equipment, leaks through sound barriers, flanking, crosstalk through ducts, and so on, there are some very basic problems inherent in the school complex, whether it is a single building or a group. Tight packing of classrooms that presents a challenge for privacy of individual classes is a major concern. Besides classrooms of the normal size (600 square feet or so) there may be offices, large lecture rooms (perhaps an auditorium/theater), laboratories, gymnasiums, and so on. Some of these special uses are described in other sections of this chapter. The discussion here will be limited to problems of the typical small classroom (elementary and high school size).

The two principal problems to be dealt with for classrooms are the sound conditions in the room that make listening to the teacher possible from all points in the room and effective separation for sound privacy in individual classrooms. There is also a possibility for incoming noises from outdoor activities or noisy corridors.

Classroom forms are typically dictated by the range of type of class to be accommodated, but for various practical reasons the typical classroom often has a simple rectangular plan and a generally cubical interior form. Some ordinary modifications can improve sound conditions in general. Carpet rather than tile or hardwood surfaces on the floor will have a general quieting effect, including noises from movements of furniture and feet. Since the room is small, any reinforcement should consider the primary effectiveness of the direct sound of the teacher's voice. Acoustical treatment of ceilings may have a general quieting effect but can substantially reduce the significant reflections for support of hearing tasks by those students farthest from the teacher.

Walls commonly present some relatively fixed situations with regard to sound reflection and absorption. One wall typically contains a significant amount of window glazing. At least one other wall is often significantly covered by chalkboard. The windows and chalkboards are hard reflectors and make for a pretty general "live" condition. This may be offset partially, however, by the other walls that typically have a lot of "stuff" on them: pinups, tackboards, shelves, hanging clothes, floppy maps, and so on. Architectural manipulations may not be able to alter this much for sound conditioning.

It is hard to tune such a room for optimal conditions. What helps a teacher with a booming, low-range voice may be redundant and may work against the quieter, higher-range voices of small children. Elaborate schemes for optimizing a single situation (teacher speaking at front of room, for example) may be thwarted by a teacher who mostly walks around while talking or prefers a circular seating arrangement of the movable chairs or desks. Most of the efforts to make the room quiet so that the crescendo of sound from all the room occupants talking at once is not deafening can work to make listening in the far reaches of the room difficult. This is to say that any major effort for sound control may be better spent on the problems of incoming noise and sound privacy between adjacent classrooms.

Isolation for sound privacy should concentrate on what is likely to be most distracting. Suppressing sounds from outdoors can be frustrated if windows are left open for natural ventilation a significant number of days of the year that the classroom is used. This is a different matter in northern Minnesota than in southern California from September to May in the typical school year.

Corridor noise is likely to come primarily through doors, and unless they can be made sound transmission resistive, other efforts will be questionably effective. If the HVAC system requires air circulation through the door, the game for sound separation is pretty much over. Nevertheless, the construction of the interior wall between the corridor and the classroom should be studied for maximum transmission resistance.

A major incoming noise source most likely to be distracting is the sound of voices in adjacent rooms. If these can be heard with any acuity, they will distract the listeners (students) from hearing the teacher in their classroom or from concentrating on study tasks. To the extent possible, efforts to block incoming noise should concentrate on the critical frequency band for the human voice. Of course, the standard STC ratings actually do this, so using them is really probably sufficient.

A real myth is the supposed sound-separating movable wall. This may work for exhibition halls, but almost never functions adequately for sound privacy of adjacent classrooms. Ask any teacher who has experience with them. Forget it—nailed-up construction or nothing!

8.5   OFFICES

Offices range considerably in occupant functions, in size, in number of occupants, and in arrangement in building planning. Here we treat only a few of the most typical problems for sound control. One issue is that of the basic building construction. To show some range, we consider first the case of a small, one-story building, most likely to be of simple wood-frame construction.

Figure 8.9 shows a small, one-story building with a flat roof. The general details of the construction are shown on Figure 8.10. These reveal the structure to be a light wood frame with structural plywood siding on the rear and ends and brick veneer on the front. The floor is a concrete

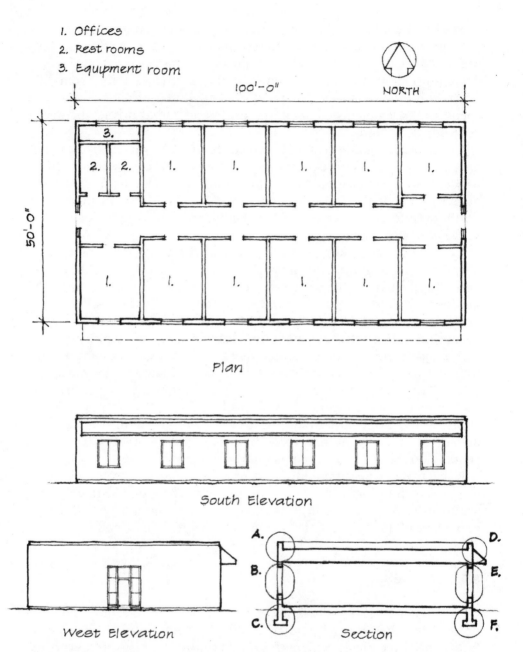

1. Offices
2. Rest rooms
3. Equipment room

100'-0"

NORTH

50'-0"

Plan

South Elevation

West Elevation

Section

A.
B.
C.
D.
E.
F.

FIGURE 8.9 One-story commercial building. A major problem here can be the amount of building skin in proportion to interior volume. If exterior sound is a major concern (traffic, aircraft, noisy neighbors, etc.), you will have to spend a lot for attenuation of the building shell before you need to worry about noise from interior situations. With light construction and most of the same services as those in the single-family house, most of the comments made for Figure 8.1 through 8.8 also apply here. If more than one tenant occupies the building, significant separation between units may be desired.

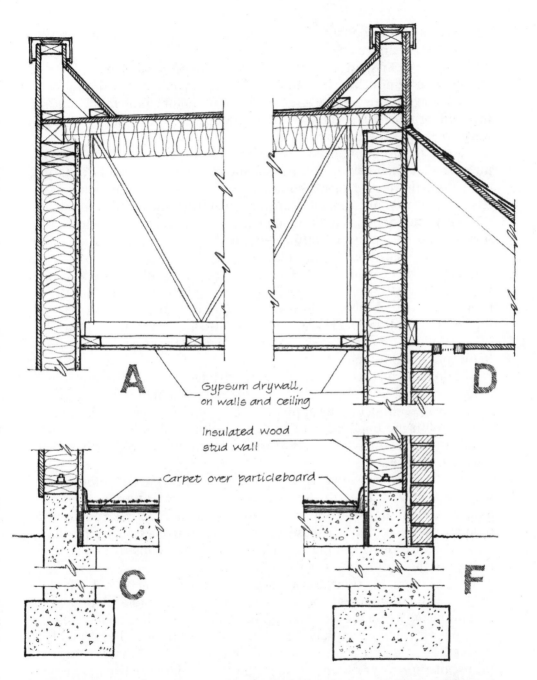

Gypsum drywall, on walls and ceiling

Insulated wood stud wall

Carpet over particleboard

FIGURE 8.10 Light wood frame, long-span roof structure. The low-density, low-insulative, leaky construction makes for a handicapped start for sound control. A lot can be done, but careful study of all factors and concentration on really feasible and significant modifications is advised. The attic space can help as a buffer for exterior sound but can be short-circuited by penetrations for lighting, plumbing vents, rooftop HVAC equipment, and so on. It can also serve as a flanking source if continuous over all the interior spaces. The common concrete slab-on-grade will carry structure-borne sound to flank separating walls; a soft joint is the only solution (see Figure 8.13).

pavement and the roof structure consists of a plywood deck on closely spaced clear-span trusses.

Use of the clear-span roof structure permits interior walls to be placed at will, with remodeling for other desired arrangements in the future easily achieved. This form of structure is common for commercial buildings built primarily as speculative rental properties, as it allows for a wide range of prospective tenants.

Despite the accommodation of interior rearrangements, certain features become relatively fixed and not subject to easy change. Primary elements in this regard are the building foundations and major structure. Also difficult to change are locations, general forms, and framing for windows and exterior doors, making some reasonably accommodating locations the most desirable. Plumbing—particularly sewer lines beneath the concrete floor slab—is also hard to change.

Changes will be made easier if most services are installed in walls or in the space above the ceiling. This will allow for major reworking of the distribution of wiring, ducts, and various items for the building power, lighting, communication, and HVAC systems. It also means that there are a lot of possibilities for sound leaks and duct-channeled crosstalk, both initially and in future remodeling.

The prefabricated trusses can be formed to have a flat bottom chord but a sloping top one to accommodate the roof drainage. For the simplest construction, the ceiling may be applied directly to the bottom chords of the trusses. With the open webs of the trusses, this still allows for major elements, such as ducts, to run perpendicular to the trusses within the ceiling interstitial space.

If partition walls do not extend into the space between the bottom and top chords of the trusses, this space becomes a large, continuous *plenum* and an excellent flanking opportunity for sound travel between adjacent rooms. Real separation will require either extension of a solid wall to the bottom of the roof deck or the use of a highly resistive construction (STC rating) for the ceiling of any space affected.

The basic construction shown for this building is quite typical, allowing for regional differences. This is a small building in total floor area, permitting the use of the light wood frame by most building codes. However, the construction may have to develop a one-hour fire rating, depending on the occupancy or on zoning requirements. If the plan were larger, the use of a sprinkler system or the placing of a separating fire wall may still allow the light wood frame to be used.

Depending on the types of occupancy, this building might be developed with no ceiling, exposing the overhead roof structure. This is less likely to occur if any interior partitioning is used, as extending partitions into the truss construction is quite messy. The various problems of dealing with exposed, overhead construction are discussed more fully in other building examples in this chapter.

The general form and some details for the HVAC system are shown in Figure 8.11. The system shown is an all-air, single-duct system using the ceiling interstitial space as a plenum return. The air-handling equipment is installed on the roof. Heating is generated by a hot water boiler that supplies piped hot water to a fan coil system. Chilled water is similarly supplied by a refrigeration system.

In this building the water heater and chilled water systems are housed in a room at floor level, which is accessed from the exterior (see Figure 8.9). The chilled water system normally uses a heat-dissipating unit that must be exposed to outdoor air, requiring it to be placed outside the building—on the roof or at ground level.

Selection of the basic HVAC system, the individual elements of the system, and the general operation of the system must respond to many concerns, principal of which are the following:

The local climate, concerning the range of temperatures, predominant concerns for heating or cooling, prevailing humidity, and wind conditions

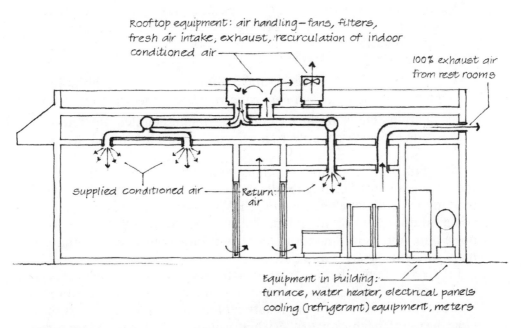

FIGURE 8.11   The HVAC system. See all the comments made for Figure 8.4. Use of the ceiling space as a common plenum return guarantees flanking and crosstalk problems. Use of the hallway as a return requires air holes through room doors, making sound-proofing between rooms and hall virtually impossible. Building service equipment must usually be either rooftop or in a room or both, making separation for distance and elimination of structure-borne noise a problem. Use planning intelligently if possible; place units over or next to spaces least affected: toilets, hallways, stairs, storerooms, and so on. Remember the neighbors if they are close by.

Planning concerns for the building, regarding the type of occupants, need for many individual controls (single interior spaces), concerns for noise and vibration of equipment, and the need for concealing of equipment—both inside and outside

Specific forms of construction, concerning particularly provision of wall and/or ceiling interstitial space, ease of access of hidden elements for maintenance or alteration, and natural thermal responses of the construction

Desired locations for equipment and for ducts, registers, controls, and so on

For the system as shown here, some specific concerns that relate to the construction are the following:

Support of the rooftop equipment and separation or isolation for control of vibration and noise. This becomes more critical when the roof structure is long-span and when the equipment is directly above noise-sensitive interior spaces.

Accommodation of the ducts, registers, and return grilles in the ceiling construction and the roof/ceiling interstitial space. This may critically affect the choice of the whole roof and ceiling construction systems.

Accommodation of the heating and chilling equipment in the building interior as a space assignment concern and a noise separation issue.

Installation details for the piping of the hot and chilled water and for wiring for electrical power and electrical signal control systems.

Use of the light wood frame with its hollow stud walls and the trussed roof with suspended ceiling results in considerable potential for accommodation of hidden elements of the HVAC system. However, this construction does not provide much help for passive thermal response or noise and vibration separation, requiring some considerable enhancement where these are major concerns.

Figure 8.12 shows the construction at the rest rooms. The wall between the rest rooms and the adjacent office is enhanced for sound separation. Some of the details for accommodation of the plumbing are also shown. Note the use of the thickened wall where wall-mounted fixtures are placed on opposite sides of the same wall.

Lighting for this building will probably be provided by four separate—although interactive—systems. These are:

A daylight-using system, using light from windows, glazed exterior doors, and—possibly—from skylights or roof windows.

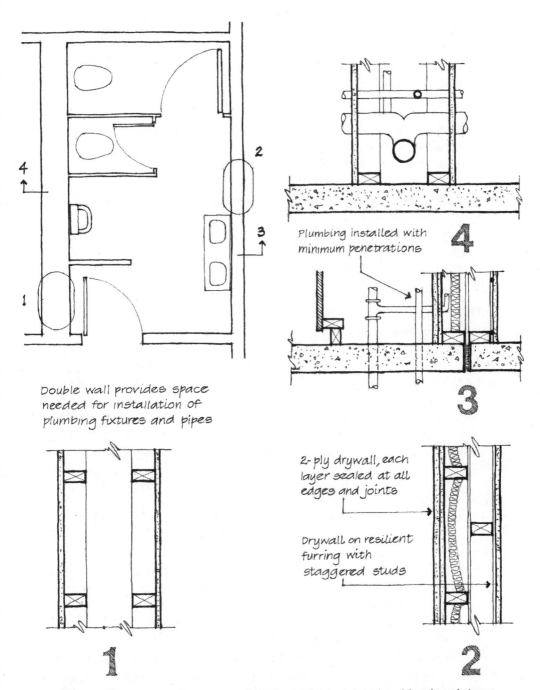

Double wall provides space
needed for installation of
plumbing fixtures and pipes

Plumbing installed with
minimum penetrations

2-ply drywall, each
layer sealed at all
edges and joints

Drywall on resilient
furring with
staggered studs

FIGURE 8.12 Construction at rest rooms. The principal sound problem here is transmission from the rest room adjacent to an office. Shown in the plan and details are the following: (1) Placing of flushing toilets on a wall other than the shared wall with the office. (2) Keeping as much piping as possible out of the shared wall. (3) Enhancing the shared wall to attenuate the barrier—with separate stud frames, sound insulation, and a soft joint in the concrete slab. Not shown: (4) Run the double-thickness drywall all the way to the underside of the roof deck to seal the barrier from the general plenum space. (5) Seal all edges, all electrical outlets, and other penetrations of the double-thickness drywall. (6) Place a continuous caulking bead under the stud wall sills. In addition, ducts for the HVAC and rest-room exhaust should be developed to avoid crosstalk between the two rest rooms.

Permanent, hard-wired fixtures, mostly for entry areas, exterior lighting, rest rooms, equipment rooms, and any permanent interior corridors.

A semipermanent, general illumination system, typically installed in response to needs of individual tenants or as a component of a general interior design development of the ceiling or other user-responsive interior construction. This system must respond to the same code requirements as the permanent elements but is usually subject to modification.

A serendipitous, expedient, instantly changeable, user-installed system using movable units (floor lamps, desk lamps, etc.) and plugged into the general electrical outlet system.

The designers of the original, basically permanent building construction have control over the choices and details for these systems more or less in descending order of their listing above. Windows and skylights are essentially permanent; desk lamps and floor lamps are almost totally out of the range of control. Still, the use of the entire array of lighting elements must be anticipated.

As with the HVAC system, the construction here is quite accommodating for installation of various forms of ordinary fixtures. For the movable, user-installed lighting—as well as for other electrical power needs—some electrical outlets must be provided in the interior construction, notably the interior partition walls. As these walls can be only partly anticipated in terms of location and form, some thought must be given to the means for installation of wiring, outlets, lighting switches, and so on. Here the most likely means for wiring of interior, movable partitions would be from the ceiling down through the hollow walls.

A sprinkler system and a smoke alarm system may be required, as well as other firefighting and alarm systems, because of local codes or simply in response to building owner or tenant requests. This construction is obviously highly combustible and fast-burning, so any help in this area will greatly enhance fire safety in general.

For this building, with the plan layout shown, a major sound control issue is the privacy of individual offices. This can be a problem for both protection from disturbing noises and maintenance of secured sound privacy. Ordinary construction of partitions in this situation is not likely to achieve much sound separation or privacy. If better performance is required, a lot of effort is required to deal with all the potential issues: enhancement of the basic wall construction, extension of the top of the wall at the ceiling level, elimination of sources for leaks and flanking, and so on.

All of this is made more difficult in the speculative-rental building. Changes in tenants will certainly require some plan modifications for the interior, so alterations of a permanent nature are not feasible. For example, the desired detail for elimination of structure-borne sound under a partition on a concrete slab (see Figure 8.13) with a joint in the slab is not realistic if the partition is classed as movable. However, a separate floor could be floated on an acoustical-separating element if the expense can be justified by the tenant.

The potential for planning for sound control is also limited. However, to the extent possible the location of the interior equipment room and the rooftop equipment should be one that anticipates the best conditions for general occupancy. Here the equipment room was placed behind the rest rooms at least partly for that reason. The rooftop units might be placed over the equipment room and rest rooms rather than centrally in the roof plan, the relatively small building here making that feasible.

General reduction of structure-borne sounds here are most likely to be achieved by isolating the sources (and if necessary, the listeners) from the structure as much as possible. However, there is a general lack of continuity in the wood frame with its many joints, so this is probably not a major issue for this building. It is greatly overshadowed by the problems of sound transmission through the light, leaky interior construction.

Multistory Office Buildings

For the single-story building the primary construction design for sound control focuses on interior partitioning and individual exterior windows. For the multistory building some different construction is to be expected as well as the added concerns for the floor/ceiling construction as a barrier between the multiple levels. For some range of consideration we will use two examples of basic construction, illustrating some variation of situations for general development of sound control.

Shown in Figures 8.14 and 8.15 is a steel frame structure with W sections used for columns, girders, and beams and a formed sheet steel deck used for the floors and roof. Many variations are possible with this basic system, dealing primarily with choices for the deck system and the members that support the deck directly.

The wall system here is a curtain wall developed as an infill steel stud system. Windows consist of horizontal strips between columns, framed into rough openings in the stud wall structure, not unlike the basic method used for single-story buildings. Details of the basic enclosure system and the floor/ceiling system at the level of the office floors are shown in Figure 8.15.

It is common to use some basic modular planning in this type of building. Spacing of the building columns constitutes one large unit in this regard but ordinarily leaves a wide range for smaller divisions. Modular coordination may also be extended to development of ceiling construction, lighting, ceiling HVAC elements, fire sprinklers, and the systems for access to electric power, phones, and other signal wiring systems.

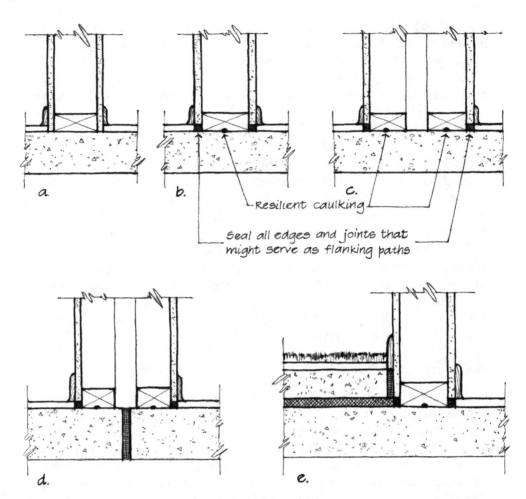

Resilient caulking

Seal all edges and joints that
might serve as flanking paths

FIGURE 8.13 Sound attenuation of the stud wall. (a) Typical wood stud wall with drywall paneling and a wood sill bolted to a supporting concrete slab. The wall itself is reasonably sound transparent, but the normal leaks at the edges of the drywall and beneath the sill guarantee almost no barrier to sound transmission (in the lowest range in Table 6.1). As shown at (b), notable improvement can be made simply by caulking the edges of the drywall and laying down a bead of caulking on the slab before the sill is bolted; however, the basic barrier is still unimproved. A significant improvement in the barrier is achieved if totally separate stud frames, not touching each other, are provided for the two wall faces (c); however, the slab remains as a structural path. Decoupling the slabs under the two rooms requires a full joint with soft separating material (d). If the continuous slab cannot be jointed, as in the case of upper floors with spanning slabs, an alternative is to use a floating floor under one or both spaces (e). Other possible improvements not shown: double-thickness drywall on one face, resilient furring for one wall face, running the drywall to the underside of the overhead structure to cut off flanking, sealing all penetrations. Testing STC values are available for just about every imaginable combination.

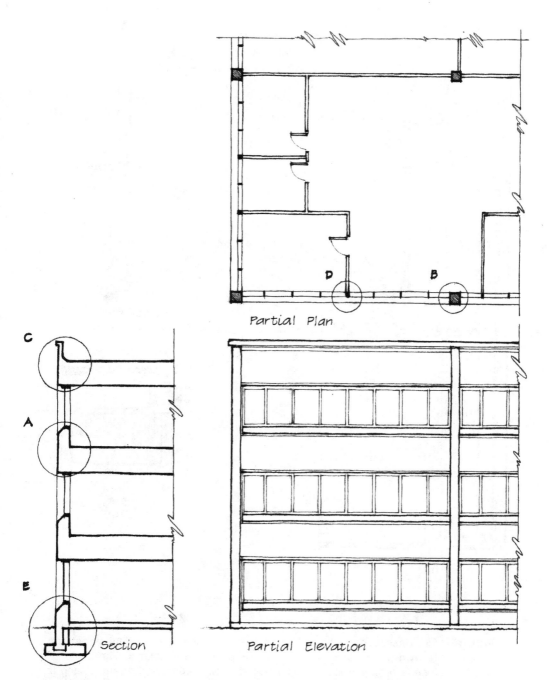

Partial Plan

Section

Partial Elevation

FIGURE 8.14 Multistory office building, punched windows in framed exterior wall. Interior finish of rooms should be developed for quiet spaces using carpet, sound-conditioning ceilings, and whatever can be used to absorb the usual high level of background noise. The floor/ceiling construction probably does not need much help as a barrier, except where penetrations for piping or electrical conduit may cause leaks. Interior partitioning is another matter, and effective isolation is a challenge. As with the one-story building, the ceiling plenum is an open opportunity for flanking.

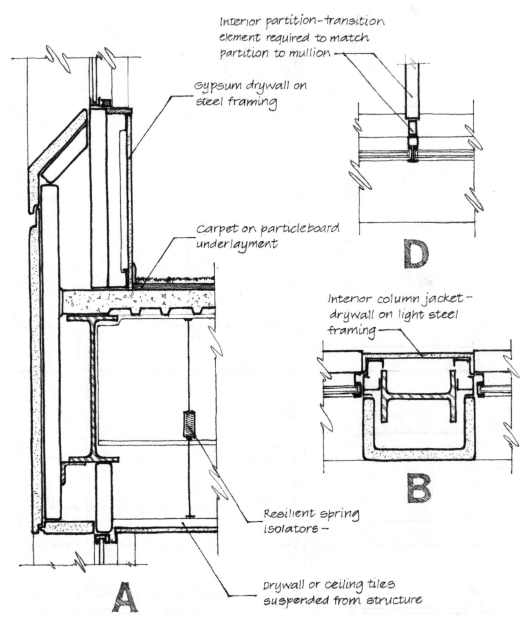

Interior partition-transition
element required to match
partition to mullion

Gypsum drywall on
steel framing

Carpet on particleboard
underlayment

Interior column jacket –
drywall on light steel
framing

D

B

A

Resilient spring
isolators –

Drywall or ceiling tiles
suspended from structure

FIGURE 8.15 Basic construction for the multistory office building. The carpet and concrete fill provide reasonable separation and impact noise resistance. The floor construction alone is probably sufficient for floor-to-floor separation, so the ceiling is redundant. However, the ceiling becomes important where noises originate in the space between the ceiling and the structure above. The steel frame is extremely efficient for structure-borne vibrations, so all major vibration sources should be decoupled from it. Without some extra attention, the windows will be quite transparent for exterior sound; get some help from the window manufacturer for special treatment for this. Detail D presents a real challenge for stopping sound leaks; do not use this where sound privacy is really critical. Although not shown, an interior partition at the column jacket offers more opportunity for sealing of leaks.

Most proprietary ceiling systems and corresponding lighting systems use the 1 foot–2 foot–4 foot system for basic elements. However, 4-foot elements can be spaced on 5-foot centers or otherwise utilized in other planning modules. Selection of a particular manufacturer's system for interior development may establish some criteria for this planning.

For buildings built as investment properties, with speculative occupancies that vary over the life of the building, it is usually desirable to accommodate future redevelopment of the building interior with some ease. For the basic construction, this means a design with as few permanent structural elements as possible. At a bare minimum, what is usually required is construction of the major structure (columns, floors, roof), exterior enclosing walls, and interior walls around stairs, elevators, rest rooms, equipment rooms, and risers for building services. Preferably, everything else should be nonstructural and easily demountable, if possible.

Figure 8.16 shows the general scheme and some details for the HVAC system for the office areas. A ceiling-mounted air system delivers air through registers that are integrated with the general modular ceiling system. Return air to the circulating system is pulled through the ceiling using the enclosed, interstitial space between the ceiling and the structure above as a general plenum space (one big duct). Air also enters this space from grilles in the corridors.

The air-handling equipment and heat-dissipating units for the air-conditioning system are located on the rooftop. Supply and return air for the offices is fed through a vertical duct shaft in the building core. The air-conditioning chiller and the furnace and hot water boiler are in the partial basement at the building core. Hot and cold water are circulated between the basement and the equipment on the rooftop through pipe chases in the core.

Another system fed by the hot water system consists of fin tube radiators along the outside walls. These are installed in the hollow space in the walls beneath the windows and feed up through grilles in the windowsills, providing a wash of warm air up the inside surface of the windows. This reduces condensation and frosting on the windows during cold weather and generally adds an extra dose of heat at the cold outside walls.

As with other buildings, special systems may be provided for HVAC service of other building space. The building rest rooms will probably have a continuously operating ventilation exhaust system, with undercut or louvered doors pulling air in from corridors to assure a one-way airflow between rest rooms and their connecting corridors.

The building core is a busy spot, with risers for the various service systems as well as the rest rooms, stairs, and elevators. Tight planning and coordination of design work is required here, with many separate designers having concerns for the space use.

Sound conditioning of individual spaces in this building will be achieved by some efforts aimed generally at the overall construction and

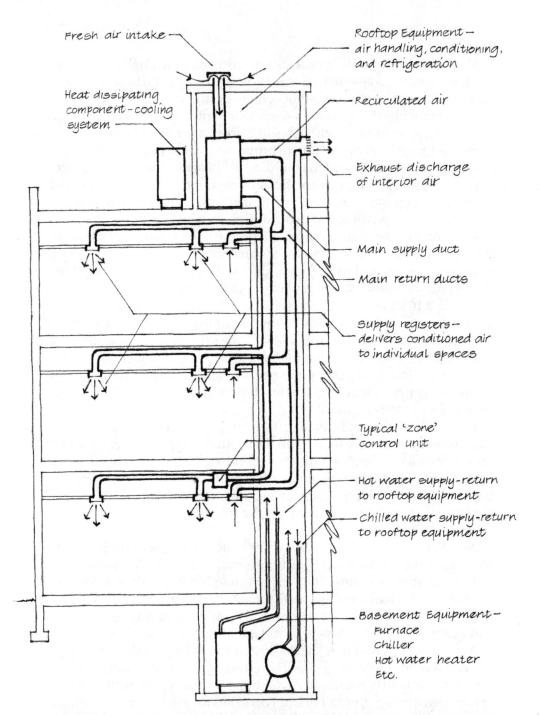

Fresh air intake

Rooftop Equipment — air handling, conditioning, and refrigeration

Heat dissipating component - cooling system

Recirculated air

Exhaust discharge of interior air

Main supply duct

Main return ducts

Supply registers — delivers conditioned air to individual spaces

Typical 'zone' control unit

Hot water supply-return to rooftop equipment

Chilled water supply-return to rooftop equipment

Basement Equipment — Furnace Chiller Hot water heater Etc.

FIGURE 8.16 HVAC system for the multistory building. See the comments for the one-story building in Figure 8.11; most apply here. Air volume and velocity in main ducts are higher here, so noise may be more critical. The vertical duct shaft can carry noise to the occupied floors from both the rooftop and basement unless an effort is made to block it. The general ceiling plenum should not be used for return air if sound privacy for separate rooms on a single floor is a priority goal. Duct crosstalk is also a potential problem in this regard.

some individually pursued for each space. Conditioning of the general construction is largely a matter for the building designers and should be provided for in the original construction. Conditioning of individual spaces—achieved by choices for flooring, ceilings, interior partitioning, and perhaps by shaping of interior spaces—will be done primarily by the designers who customize the interior for individual building tenants.

The building designers must do their best to anticipate what the interior designers may want to do for different situations and provide for a range of possibilities. The interior designers pretty much have to deal with what they get unless they are included in the original project design team for the building.

The needs, desires, and pocketbooks of tenants will establish individual design goals for the interior design work. A lot can be done if necessary, even with the handicap of starting with little or no design effort for sound control by the designers of the building. Floors can be floated on sound-absorbing materials; partitions can be developed with significant STC values and general sound-blocking effectiveness; ceilings can be developed for major effects on room acoustics; doors can be made to create high levels of privacy and noise reduction.

However, the general building design can also possibly give the interior designers a head start. Choices for floor decks and the general floor/ceiling construction can include some considerations for acoustical properties. Design of the exterior walls can achieve some major reduction of incoming noise where this is a potential problem—on busy streets, near airports, next door to some noisy industrial activity, and so on. Selection of the basic products for development of the glazed portions of the walls may include requirements for acoustic performance.

A major potential source for noises and possibilities for sound leaks, flanking, and crosstalk is the building HVAC system. This includes noisy items of equipment, transmission paths through ductwork, and leaks through the many penetrations made by ducts, piping, and wiring. Considerations for better sound conditions in these regards are best made in the original design and carefully assured by thorough inspections during the construction work. Any necessary remedial work is likely to be difficult and expensive, if not actually unfeasible.

Sound-conscious design of the exterior walls becomes even more critical if a full curtain wall system is used. Figure 8.17 shows a form of construction using such a wall system that wraps the entire building exterior. This typically also adds greater concerns for leaks through the floor-to-exterior wall joint, a location for great concern for fire as well as sound leaks. The choice for a fully glazed exterior elevates the choices of materials and details for the wall system to major concerns for control of exterior noise.

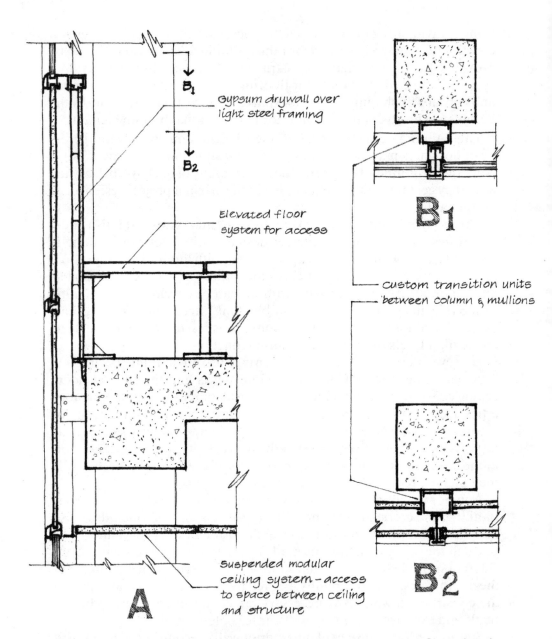

Gypsum drywall over light steel framing

B₁

Elevated floor system for access

custom transition units between column & mullions

B₂

Suspended modular ceiling system – access to space between ceiling and structure

A

FIGURE 8.17 Alternative construction for the multistory office building. Shown here is a concrete frame with a continuous metal-framed curtain wall hung outside the structure. This wall is even more vulnerable for exterior sounds, and some data and help should be sought from the manufacturer. Sound leaks at the spandrel are possible, but some insulation will be used here for fire safety, so it may solve the problem. The elevated floor adds extra separation, especially for the concrete slab, which can create a problem with impact noises (see Figure 7.1). The detail at the connection between the curtain wall and the column needs study for sound leaks.

Figure 8.17 shows another spot where sound leaks can be critical. This is at the joint between the exterior wall and the building columns, which is often likely to be a location for interior partitions between rooms. (See details B1 and B2 in Figure 8.17.) This detail might be altered by interior designers, but good details can also be created in the original building design.

Figures 8.17 and 8.18 also show the use of an elevated floor system. This may add to sound separation between levels, although its contribution may be redundant in many cases. However, Figure 8.18 shows a situation where no suspended ceiling is used in the interior development, leaving the underside of the concrete structure exposed. This is a common situation in apartments and hotels but not so much in offices. In apartments and hotels the higher acoustic separation desired is usually attained by modifications of the floor treatment on top of the structure. The same thing can be done for the office building, but the use of the elevated floor here might make that unnecessary.

8.6 STORES AND OTHER PUBLIC PLACES

Stores and other places where people congregate and mill around present various potential problems. Much depends on the size, shape, and characteristics of the space and on the number of people involved. Background noise levels may be very high during normal activities, and a major effort may be simply to lower them as much as possible. Whatever business needs to be transacted that requires people to converse, to speak on the phone, or to hear broadcast information must be dealt with over the background noise.

Besides the real need for hearing tasks, some comfort level for the occupants may be sought. General efforts may be primarily in the direction of overall reduction of reflected sounds and reduction of sound from any disturbing noise sources. A generally relaxed, soothing ambient environmental condition may be a primary goal.

For large spaces careful study should be made of reverberations and special problems of standing waves, echoes, and so on. This is a place where some expertise is useful and the services of an experienced acoustics consultant might be indicated if sound is considered to be important. All the discussions for room acoustics as developed in Chapter 6 can be applied, but specific goals may take expert analysis to achieve.

8.7 RESTAURANTS

Desired sound conditions for restaurants, bars, and similar establishments very considerably. A German beer hall or New York deli would not

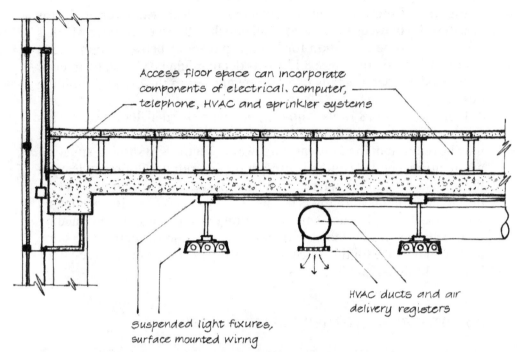

Access floor space can incorporate
components of electrical, computer,
telephone, HVAC and sprinkler systems

HVAC ducts and air
delivery registers

Suspended light fixtures,
surface mounted wiring

FIGURE 8.18   Development of the multistory floor/ceiling construction without a suspended ceiling. This involves an interior design with either a raw, bare-bones look or a very high-tech style. Without the ceiling all noises from ducts, recirculation units with fans, and lighting ballasts will become full components of the room background noise level. Also of possible concern may be impact floor noise from above—probably not in this case with the elevated floor, but certainly without it and and a hard floor finish above.

be realistic without a steady din for background noise; a night spot with a jazz band or rap group is a study in thresholds of pain for hearing.

Let us assume that an ordinary eating establishment desires a relaxed, peaceful atmosphere, the ability of patrons to carry on relatively private conversations without yelling, and the ability of the waiters to hear the customers orders distinctly—giving a 50/50 chance of getting it right. Added background noise of the pink variety (elevator music, etc.) may be used here partly to mask more annoying sounds or provide some privacy for individual groups.

Otherwise, any of the usual tricks for reducing reflections, controlling reverberations, and eliminating undesired noises can be used. With a large crowd all talking at once, incoming noises may be insignificant; reverberation and standing waves may really be critical for some room sizes and shapes. Tuning the room to the degree possible to suppress the dull roar originating inside may be a principal design goal.

Surely a carpeted floor, a multiplaned and highly absorptive ceiling, upholstered furniture, thick linen tableclothes, and some fabric hangings on the walls may help considerably, as may some good planning and treatments of the sound paths from the kitchen and parking lots. Beyond that it may be more productive to deal with the broadcast sound system and the choice for the background music.

8.8 SPORTS FACILITIES

Enclosures for sports facilities very considerably. There is not much architectural design variation that can be accomplished for a handball court, but there are some possibilities for bowling alleys, roller skating rinks, and enclosed stadiums for various sports. Concerns for sound are often not addressed so much to the players as to groups of spectators or persons in nearby spaces with sound privacy or listening task goals. For background, the roar of the crowd may be a stimulus to the players—and to the crowd, for that matter. But being able to hear the crack of the bat, grunts of the players, and other sounds of the play action, as well as announcements from the broadcast sound system, may well provide some goals for sound control.

The room is often likely to be large here, and reverberations, echoes, and other phenomena may well be of some concern. Some means may be available for controlling them, but many design choices are likely to be dictated by the spatial needs and other requirements for the sports. You just cannot carpet a basketball court.

Acoustics may be a factor in the choices for surface materials, the form of the overhead structure, or the building plan in general, but is likely to take a back seat with respect to economy, spectator sight lines, spatial needs for the sports activities, fire exits, maintenance, and many other considerations. It may well be necessary to deal with sound pretty much in a remedial fashion, after design choices are fixed from other goals and criteria and an untenable condition is discovered after occupancy.

General data and guidelines for the large enclosure can be used here with problems shared with other large places of assembly. In fact, many large rooms will be asked to serve a range of uses, including concerts, ceremonies, large meetings, dances, and so on, in addition to general use for athletic purposes. For sound as well as other concerns, this will provide some range of desired performance requirements, and some ranked order of importance of usage may be necessary. What wants to be served the best? Everything, of course, but realism and practicality may require some compromises.

Modifications of various kinds might be made in adapting for different functions. Besides the rearranging of seating and other actions, these might include the placing of movable elements for sound control that seriously affect reverberations, reinforce certain sound sources and frequencies, or otherwise adjust the sound responses of the room. For this, the true optimal conditions for each contemplated usage can be studied and any means to obtain them explored in terms of modifiable conditions. Adjustments of movable acoustic panels at the ceiling can become as routine as the modifications of seating, entry and exit control, and other routine modifications for different uses.

8.9   AUDITORIUMS, THEATERS, AND CHURCHES

Large places of assembly have major problems for room acoustics. This is not an area of design for amateurs. In many cases the problem is made more complex by the use of amplified sound systems that interact with the room's basic structural and form responses. Basic usages and typical constructions are created repeatedly, so that a lot of experience can be brought to bear on new designs. Still, the number of variables alone indicates the need for an expert to evaluate and implement them for any design work. Get the best acoustic consultant you can find and afford.

We confine our attention here to a simple example—a small church building with a single, auditorium-like space and fixed seating. Figure 8.19 shows a single-space, medium-span building with essentially no interior structure. The options possible for this building in terms of type of structure and architectural style are virtually endless. Shown here is a popular form of construction, with gabled bents of glued laminated wood and an exposed wood beam and plank deck roof. Exterior infill walls between the gabled bents are achieved with light wood-frame construction.

The general forms of the building and the vaulted interior are shown in Figure 8.19. The front podium/altar area is slightly raised as a stepped platform. The other end of the church may well contain some rooms and a balcony with an entry area and stairs, but we deal only with the auditorium portion of the building shown here.

The basic construction of the building shell is shown in the details in Figure 8.20. The building interior is comprised primarily of the insides of the roof and exterior walls and the top of the concrete pavement. Further development of the interior consists mostly of choices for the finishes on these elements.

With the exposed form of construction for the roof, there is no suspended ceiling or other form of interstitial space in the upper portion of the auditorium. This poses some severe limitations on the systems for HVAC and lighting, especially if general concealment of the installation is desired. A general overhead ducted HVAC system is out of the question unless the entire thing can be hung out for display. This is possible, of course, but does not fit well with this interior and general construction.

Other options for the HVAC system for the auditorium depend somewhat on local climate and the overall use of the building. Churches are often used only at certain times, so a system may be able to be shut down—

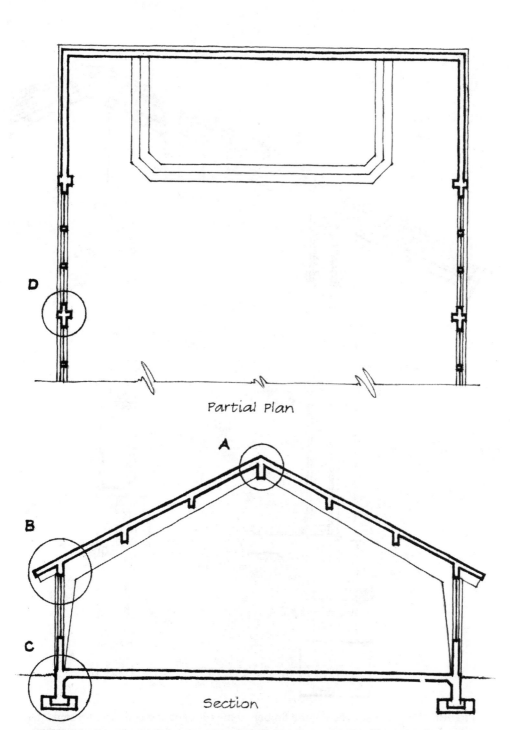

Partial Plan

Section

FIGURE 8.19 Form of the church/auditorium without interior space division. This is a one-story building and the admonitions regarding the ratio of exterior shell to building volume apply as discussed for the one-story commercial building (Figure 8.9). There is a lot of exterior shell to be attenuated for sound here. The principal sound problems are the interior room acoustics (for both speech and music), possibility of intrusion of outside noise, and possibility for duct or HVAC equipment noise.

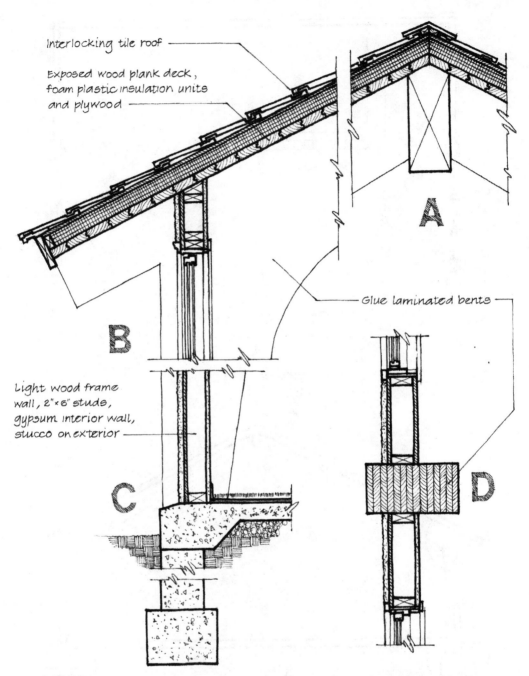

Interlocking tile roof

Exposed wood plank deck,
foam plastic insulation units
and plywood

Glue laminated bents

Light wood frame
wall, 2"×6" studs,
gypsum interior wall,
stucco on exterior

A

B

C

D

FIGURE 8.20 Construction of the timber-frame roof and the light wood-frame infill walls. The roofs is reasonably sound opaque with its insulation and multiple layers, but the walls are quite transparent in their "natural" state and need a lot of improvement to reduce the transmission of exterior noise to any significant degree. With the exposed wood plank roof deck, drywall, and window glass, the ceiling and walls will have low absorption, so reverberation may be a little high—good for music perhaps but poor for speech audibility. The minister may need the help of an amplified system.

or at least operate at limited capacity—for extended periods. However, when the space is to be used, it is usually desired to bring it to a comfort level fairly quickly, a performance best had from an all-air system. If the space sees a lot of ongoing use, however (for church, school, and general social activities), it needs a system that is similar to that for other buildings with regular usage.

A possibility for an all-air system is shown in Figure 8.21, employing underfloor ducts that feed perimeter floor-level registers. The registers may be in the floor, as shown, or possibly in the wall beneath the windows. A variation on this would be to have the registers high in the walls, possibly above the windows, which would work somewhat better for delivering air to the center of the space. Assuming a freestanding building and use primarily for church services, the concerns for sound control are primarily those described below.

Exterior Noise

The exterior wall construction shown is really sound porous (noninsulative, leaky) and should get some attention for improvements if there are potential exterior noisy conditions (busy streets or other on-site or nearby activities). In cold weather climates the general efforts to obtain a better insulative and air-sealed building exterior will help a lot for sound. Use of a masonry veneer or solid masonry instead of the wood-frame wall would greatly improve things for the solid wall portions.

However, the windows are really the major sound-leaking and transmission problem. The only way to make them remotely resistive to sound transmission is to use fixed glazing in well-sealed frames. If this is done and the window area is a small part of the total wall, and the windows are placed high on the wall (above the heads of the people) and perhaps laminated glazing with sound-reducing properties is used, some significant reduction of incoming noise may be achieved.

Background Noise

With the hard surfaces for the windows, exterior wall, and underside of the roof deck, there is likely to be a significant reverberation effect. This should be investigated and the use of an amplified system should be considered, especially for help to listeners in the rear of the church. Use of a fully carpeted floor will help for most sound purposes involving reverberation and background noise. A sound-absorbing surface for the ceiling might be useful but is hardly likely with the exposed plank roof; besides, the reflections are probably helpful for listeners in the back of the church.

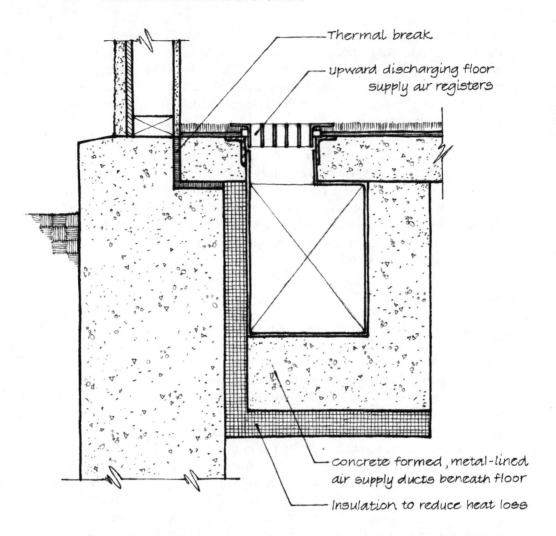

Thermal break

upward discharging floor supply air registers

concrete formed, metal-lined air supply ducts beneath floor

Insulation to reduce heat loss

FIGURE 8.21 The underfloor HVAC delivery system. This is probably relatively low-velocity air, so duct and register noise should not be a problem; nevertheless, it should be controlled in the design. The system should be designed to operate continuously during services (air blowing all the time) so that the people adjust to the constant background noise level and do not have it jerked up and down as the fans go off and on.

Duct and register noises from the HVAC system should be reduced as much as possible by choice and sizing of elements. With HVAC equipment most likely near the rear of the church, the loudest noises from these sources will probably affect the listeners the farthest from the front of the church, adding to their problems for hearing.

Building Equipment

HVAC equipment is not likely to be on the rooftop with this roof form. If equipment is inside the building—probably in the rear—it should be sound isolated for both airborne and structure-borne noise. This means some special construction and special installation details to decouple the equipment from both the rest of the building construction and from its own delivery system.

BIBLIOGRAPHY

The following list contains materials that have been used as a references in the development of various portions of the book. Also included are some widely used publications that serve as general references for design of buildings. The numbering system is random and merely serves to simplify referencing by text notation.

References for Acoustics

1. *Sound Control Construction: Principles and Performance*, 2nd ed., United States Gypsum Co., Chicago, 1972. Still one of the most concise and well-written explanations of basic principles and issues.
2. *A Guide to Airborne, Impact, and Structureborne Noise Control in Multifamily Dwellings*, U.S. Department of Housing and Urban Development, Washington, DC, 1963; prepared for the Federal Housing Administration by the National Bureau of Standards. An exhaustive source of information for data and performance of construction for typical forms of multistory buildings.
3. Benjamin Stein and John S. Reynolds, *Mechanical and Electrical Equipment for Buildings*, 8th ed., Wiley, New York, 1992. Part IX: Acoustics.
4. Cyril M. Harris, editor-in-chief, *Noise Control in Buildings*, McGraw-Hill, New York, 1994.
5. Cyril M. Harris, editor-in-chief, *Handbook of Acoustical Measurements and Noise Control*, 3rd ed., McGraw-Hill, New York, 1991.
6. M. David Egan, *Architectural Acoustics*, McGraw-Hill, New York, 1988.

General Building Design References

7. *Uniform Building Code*, 1994 ed., International Conference of Building Officials, 5360 South Workmanmill Road, Whittier, CA 90601. (Called simply the *UBC*.)

8. Charles G. Ramsey and Harold R. Sleeper, *Architectural Graphic Standards*, 9th ed., Wiley, New York, 1994.

9. Edward Allen, *Fundamentals of Building Construction: Materials and Methods*, 2nd ed., Wiley, New York, 1990.

10. James Ambrose, *Building Construction and Design*, Chapman & Hall, New York, 1992.

11. *Sweet's Catalog Files: General Building and Renovation*, Sweet's Group, McGraw-Hill, New York. Sections 09500 and 13034 have acoustic materials; many other sections for individual products (ceilings, partitions, doors, etc.) also have acoustic information.

GLOSSARY

A-Scale. Reference intended to match the response characteristics of the average human listener; called dBA.

Absorbers. Materials that have the capacity to absorb sound, such as acoustical tile and panels, carpeting, draperies, and upholstered furniture.

Absorption. Taking up and holding or dissipating of matter or energy as a sponge takes up water. Absorption is the opposite of reflection.

Acoustical Privacy. State of sufficient insulation (protection) from intruding and disturbing noise.

Acuity. Relative clarity (sharpness, keenness) of sound communication.

Ambient. Existing surrounding conditions. Ambient noise level refers to the existing condition in a space as a result of enduring sounds from all sources.

Amplitude. Measurement of sound level in wavelength terms.

Attenuation of Sound. Reduction of sound energy as it passes through a conductor, resulting from the conductor's resistance to the transmission.

Barrier (Sound). Structure that impedes direct sound transmission.

Complex Waves. Sound waves combining two or more frequencies.

Concave. Curved toward the observer: cupped.

Conductor. Material that carriers or transmits energy from one location to another. A conductor of sound must be an elastic material.

Convex. Curved away from the observer: rounded.

Criteria. Standards by which performance can be judged.

Crosstalk. Two-way exchange of sounds between spaces through a connecting sound path; usually a flanking or leaking path (connecting ducts, pipe chases, back-to-back wall fixtures, etc.).

Cycle. One complete phase of an action, such as one revolution of a wheel or one full swing of a pendulum. In relation to sound, one to-and-from movement of the vibrating object or one high–low pressure sequence of a sound wave.

Damping. Effect that reduces the amplitude of a vibration.

Decibel (dB). Unit adopted for convenience in representing vastly different sound pressures. It is 20 times the logarithm to the base 10 of the ratio of the sound pressure to a reference pressure of 0.0002 dyne/cm^2. This reference pressure is considered the lowest value that the ear can detect.

Density. Ratio of the mass (or weight) of a body to its volume. A common unit of measure is pounds per cubic foot.

Diaphragm. Thin body that separates two areas; in sound, the skin of a partition or ceiling that separates the room from the structural space in the center of the partition or ceiling assembly.

Diffraction. Change in direct that occurs when a wave contacts a space, surface, or edge smaller than the wavelength.

Diffuse. To spread out evenly and thus become less dense or concentrated.

Displacement. Forced movement away from an original location.

Dominant Pitch. Subjective response of the ear to the fundamental frequency of a sound; usually louder than the harmonic overtones and of lower frequency.

Dyne. Unit of force; specifically, the force required to accelerate 1 gram of mass 1 centimeter per second per second.

Elastic. Capacity to return to original shape after deflection.

Energy. Ability to perform work; in sound, the capacity to compress the conductor molecules.

Flanking. Taking a path around something, such as a sound barrier.

Flanking Transmission. Transmission of sounds by indirect paths; around, rather than through, intervening barriers.

Frequency. Number of times that an action occurs in a given time period. In sound, the number of complete vibration cycles per second represented by the unit hertz (Hz).

Fundamental Frquency. Dominant and usually lowest frequency of a sound which establishes the frequencies of the harmonics.

Harmonics. Secondary frequencies that are whole-number multiples of the fundamental frequency of a sound. The harmonics combine with the fundamental to produce the complex sound wave, giving timbre or quality to the total sound as perceived.

Hertz (Hz). Unit of measure of frequency, representing cycles per second.

Homogeneous. Of uniform composition and structure.

Impact Insulation Class (IIC). Whole, positive number rating, based on standardized test performance, for evaluating the effectiveness of assemblies in isolating impact sound transmission.

Intensity. Rate of sound energy passing through a unit area.

Masking (Sound). Added sound that increases the background noise level to reduce perception of incoming noises.

Mitigation. Reduction of the effect of something (general definition).

Murphy's Law. Anything that *can* go wrong *will* go wrong.

Noise. Undesired sound; usually of a disturbing nature or causing interference with some hearing task.

Noise Reduction Coefficient (NRC). Mathematical average of sound absorption coefficients recorded at the frequencies of 250, 500, 1000, and 2000 Hz.

Octave. Interval between a sound of one frequency and a sound with a frequency that is exactly double the first.

Octave Band. Frequency spectrum that is one octave wide. Bands of one-third octave are used for recording sound test results and are designated by the center frequency of the band.

Oscillogram. Graphic representations of sound waves, recorded with the aid of electronic equipment.

Overtones. Subjective response of the ear to harmonics.

Party Wall. Wall or partition separating two occupancies in a building.

Pitch. Highness or lowness of a sound as perceived by the ear. While the frequency of the sound determines the highness, pitch is the subjective response to it.

Plenum. Enclosed air space.

Pressure Waves. Layers of high and low pressure that radiate out in all directions from a sound source.

Radiate. To travel in straight lines away from a center, such as sound waves moving out from a source.

Resilient Attachment. Fastening system that reduces the transmission of vibrations.

Resonance. Sympathetic vibration of an object when subjected to a vibration of a specific frequency. The object tends to act as a sound source.

Reverberation. Continuation of sound reflections within a space after the sound source has ceased.

Sabin. Unit of measure of sound absorption; the amount of sound absorbed by a theoretically perfect absorptive surface of 1 square foot area. Named for Wallace C. W. Sabine, noted American physicist.

Sound. For our purposes: what is received by human listeners through the physiological process of hearing.

Sound Attenuation. *See* Attenuation of Sound.

Sound Conditioning. Designing and equipping a space for faithful retention of desirable sounds and maximum relief from undesirable acoustical effects.

Sound Leak. Hole or crack that permits sound to pass through a separating barrier (wall, floor, roof).

Sound Pressure. Instantaneous change in pressure resulting from vibration of the conductor in the audible frequency range. Conversational speech at close range produces a sound pressure of about 1 dyne per square centimeter.

Sound Propagation. Origination and transmission of sound energy.

Sound Transmission. Transfer of sound energy from one place to another, through air, structure, or other conductor.

Sound Transmission Class (STC). Rating based on standardized test performance for evaluating the effectiveness of assemblies in isolating airborne sound transmission.

Structure-Borne Sound (Noise). Sound imparted directly to and transmitted through the building construction.

Subjective. Related to conditions of the brain and sense organs rather than to direct physical actions.

Symmetrical. State of being identical or balanced on each side of a real or imaginary dividing line.

Timbre. Subjective response of the ear to the quality or richness of a sound, produced by the number and relative energy of the harmonics and other frequencies present in the sound.

Tone. Subjective response of the ear to the pitch of a sound.

Variable. Value that changes with changes in the conditions.

Velocity. Rate of travel.

Vibration. Uniform, rapid movement of an elastic material in a back-and-forth direction.

Watt. Unit of power. Sound pressure intensity can be directly measured in watts/cm^2 or in dynes/cm^2.

Waveform. Shape of the graphic representation of a sound wave.

Wavefront. Spherical surface of the wave as it travels out in all directions from the source.

Wavelength. Physical distance between identical points on successive waves. The wavelength is a function of the frequency and the speed of sound in the conductor.

APPENDIX: PRODUCTS FOR SOUND CONTROL

The materials on the following pages have been abstracted from information circulated by individual manufacturers of products for sound control. These materials are reproduced without commentary from the pages of publications of the manufacturers with the manufacturers' approval. Additional information and more current data are available from the individual manufacturers, whose names are given at the bottom of the pages.

Neither the authors nor the publishers of this book convey any endorsement of the products shown here. This information is given merely for the purpose of illustrating the range of current products for the readers.

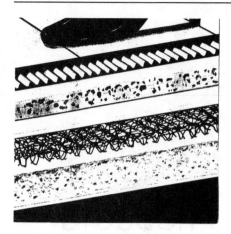

Enkasonic, sandwiched between the subflooring and a support overlay (such as a reinforced mortar bed, Wonder-Board®, Gyp-Crete® 2000, or 2 layers of plywood), now gives designers the option of using hard surface flooring where STC *and* IIC ratings must be above 50.

The Enkasonic floor system creates a "floating floor" that not only breaks the sound transmission path through the floor-ceiling assembly but also prevents lateral transmission through the floor-wall contact area.

Prior to installing Enkasonic® the perimeter of the subfloor along the baseboard area is lined with polyethylene foam (2-9 PCF) or fiberglass board (6-15 PCF) to isolate the "floating floor" and eliminate flanking noise that could be conducted through the walls. Sound suppression in Enkasonic is accomplished when the resilient nylon geomatrix converts and stores vibrational energy.

Enkasonic was designed in conjunction with the Ceramic Tile Institute (CTI) specifically for use under ceramic tile. Additional testing has demonstrated outstanding sound attenuation with a variety of construction assemblies and floor coverings, including marble, native stone, vinyl tile, parquet, and hardwood.

Long Term Performance of Enkasonic

After being installed for ten years at the historic Hermitage Condominiums on Russian Hill in San Francisco, Enkasonic was removed during a remodeling project. The ten year old Enkasonic sample was tested for resistance to long term compression, dynamic resilience and performance.

- The ten year old sample retained 97% of its original thickness.
- After ten years Enkasonic was as pliable as a new roll.
- Akzo tested samples of the older material for comparison with Enkasonic Matting produced today. Two rolls from current Akzo inventory were tested as well as several competitive products on the market. After providing a decade of service beneath a hardwood floor, the ten year old Enkasonic performed equal to the newly manufactured Enkasonic materials and better than any of the competitive products tested.

Enkasonic was again the sound barrier of choice to go under the newly remodeled hardwood floor of the Historic Hermitage Condominiums.

Enkasonic®

Sound Control Matting

Enkasonic sound control matting is a proven solution to a modern design challenge—creating code recognized floor systems that meet stringent sound ratings in multiple-story dwellings or buildings. Enkasonic effectively inhibits sound

transmission when used beneath ceramic tile, marble, wood, vinyl, or carpet flooring, in both wood frame and concrete slab construction.

Enkasonic is a 0.4" thick composite of nylon filaments forming a three-dimensional geomatrix with a nonwoven fabric heat bonded to the upper surface. The durable pliable Enkasonic obstructs transmission of sound and makes possible cost effective sound-rated floors. Because of its thin cross-section, it's ideal for new construction and retrofit, and costs less than a "built-up" floor to achieve the same sound ratings.

Before development of reasonably priced sound-rated floor systems, developers often avoided hard surfaces. It is now possible to ensure the privacy of tenants in multistory buildings with Enkasonic floor systems.

Generalized Enkasonic
Sound-Rated Floor System

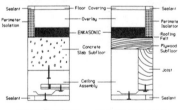

Concrete Floor System   Wood-Joist Floor System

Manufacturer: Akzo Industrial Systems Company

Sound Ratings–Tested Enkasonic Floor/Ceiling Assemblies
Concrete Floor System

Test Reference	Subfloor	Susp. Ceiling	Enkasonic Overlay	Floor Covering	Lab Tests STC	IIC
Akzo C-11	4" slab	no	7/16" Wonder-Board	tile	55	52
CTI #11	8" slab	no	7/16" Wonder-Board	tile	59	52
CTI #8	8" slab	yes	1 1/4" mortar bed	tile	61	62
CTI #12	8" slab	no	1 1/4" mortar bed	tile	60	54
AKZO C-1	8" slab	yes	1 1/4" mortar bed	vinyl tile	61	67
AKZO C-2	8" slab	yes	1 1/4" mortar bed	carpet & pad	61	79
AKZO C-3	8" slab	yes	1 1/4" mortar bed	5/16" wood parquet	61	65
AKZO C-4	8" slab	yes	2 layers—3/8" plywood (min)	3/4" T&G oak	60	61

Wood–Joist Floor System

Test Reference	Subfloor	Susp. Ceiling	Enkasonic Overlay	Floor Covering	Lab Tests STC	IIC
CTI #5	5/8" plywood	yes	7/16" Wonder-Board	tile	62	58
CTI #7	5/8" plywood	yes	1 1/4" mortar bed	tile	60	55
AKZO W-3	5/8" plywood	yes	1 1/2" Gyp-Crete® 2000[1]	tile	59	57

1. NobleSeal™ TS isolation membrane or equivalent is bonded to the Gyp-Crete 2000 prior to thinsetting the tile.
CTI listings refer to the Ceramic Tile Institute Sound-Rated Floor Systems per bulletin CTI-R5-113-79. Details about the Sound-Rated Floor Systems listed above and others are available upon request.

Installation Summary

1) The subfloor must be structurally sound. Deflection should not exceed 1/360 of the span, including live and dead loads.
2) Install polyethylene foam or fiberglass board at the perimeter of the entire subfloor and around any protrusions through the installation. This isolates the floor and breaks the sound transmission path between floor and walls. Tape or tack-glue the isolation material.
3) Enkasonic is installed with black matrix down, fabric up. Adjoining edges of the black matrix should be butted together with the fabric overlap taped or glued to the adjacent strip.
4) A cleavage membrane (4-mil polyethylene film) or 15-lb. roofing felt is recommended between Enkasonic and MORTAR BED.
5) MORTAR BED should be 1 part portland cement and 5 parts damp sand, by volume.
6) LIGHTWEIGHT CONCRETE 1800 psi, 1½" thick should be poured directly over Enkasonic. To insure proper bond, add skim coat of Consac™ mortar supported by a ⅛" fiberglass mesh.
7) When overlay is GYP-CRETE 2000, the fabric portion of the Enkasonic should be preconditioned per manufacturer's direction.
8) WONDER-BOARD should be placed on top of Enkasonic with a ¼" gap between units, taped on both sides of joints (2" coated fiberglass tape), and butt-bonded with latex portland cement bond coat.
9) PLYWOOD should be ⅜ in. for hardwood floors (⅝ in. for vinyl and carpet & pad), APA rated sheathing, with 2 layers of 90 degrees to one another, joints gapped and offset, top sheet glued (full coverage, non-water based) to bottom sheet. The two layers are fastened with screws in corners and center or with staples (1" wide crown/6" o.c.) with no penetration into the Enkasonic.
10) Bond coat for CERAMIC TILE is dry-set mortar or latex/portland cement mortar on a cured mortar bed or latex/portland cement mortar on a WONDER-BOARD installation.

Wonder-Board® is a trademark of Custom Building Products. Seal Beach, CA (800) 272-8786.

Ceramic Tile Inst. (CTI) Culver City, CA (310) 574-7800.

NobleSeal™ TS is a trademark of the Noble Co., Grand Haven. MI. (616) 842-7844.

AMCEL™ 27 is a trademark of American Excelsior Company. Arlington, TX. (817) 640-1555.

Nominal Dimensions And Weights

Material:	Nylon 6
Width:	39 in. (plus 3 in. fabric overlap)
Length:	111 ft
Area:	360 ft²
Thickness:	0.4 in.
Roll Diameter:	27 in.
Gross Roll Weight:	58 lbs.
Total Weight:	22.9 oz/yd²
Matrix Weight:	19.4 oz/yd²
Fabric Weight:	3.5 oz/yd²

Deflection

CTI approved Enkasonic Sound-Rated Floor Systems; Case #5—Enkasonic overlain by Wonder-Board.®

Pressure (psf)	Deflection (in.)
100	0.028
200	0.046
500	0.087
1000	0.131
2000	0.189
4000	0.256

Flammability   ASTM E84   NFPA Class A

Fuel Contribution	0
Flame Spread Index	15
Smoke Density	25

Standards/Guides

ICBO	ER4778
City of LA	RR25066
NY City Dept. of Bldgs.	MEA 144-89-M
Ceramic Tile Inst.	CTI-R4-113-79
Tile Council of Am. Inc.	RF 900-91

CONSAC™ is a trademark of W.W. Henry Company, Huntington Park, CA (213) 583-4961
GYP-CRETE® is a trademark of the Gyp-Crete Corp, Hamel, MN. (612) 478-6072.
STC and IIC rating for other Enkasonic sound-rated floor systems are available upon request.
Note: STC ratings done in accordance with ASTM E90 or E336 and E413.
IIC atings done in accordance with ASTM E492.
All CTI sound-rated floor systems utilizing Enkasonic have successfully met the performance requirements of ASTM C627, with ratings from residential to heavy commercial.

We believe the information contained herein to be reliable and accurate for applications of ENKASONIC®. Since conditions vary with each site, Akzo makes no guarantee of results and assumes no obligation or liability for such results, the suitability of the material or the information contained herein for the use contemplated, unless specifically made in writing by Akzo, or for safety or other damages occurring in connection with any installation. Furthermore, Akzo's liability under any claim shall be limited to the cost of the ENKASONIC materials or replacement thereof, at Akzo's option. This publication is not a license under which to operate and is not intended to suggest infringement upon or use of any existing patents or trademarks.
ENKASONIC is a registered trademark of Akzo Industrial Systems Co. and is covered by a number of U.S. patents.

QUICK SELECTOR FOR SOUND AND FIRE RATED ASSEMBLIES

Partitions/Wood Framing (load-bearing)

No.	Fire Rating		Ref.	Design No.	Description	STC	Test No.
SINGLE LAYER							
1	45 min.		UL	U317	1/2" Fire-Shield G Gypsum Wallboard nailed both sides 2 x 4 studs, 16" o.c.	34	NGC 2161
			FM	W1–45 min.			
2	1 hr.		UL	U305	5/8" Fire-Shield Gypsum Wallboard or Fire-Shield MR Board nailed on both sides 2 x 4 wood studs, 16" o.c.	35	NGC 2403
			FM	W16A–1 hr.			
			GA	WP 3605			
3	1 hr.		UL	U309	5/8" Fire-Shield Gypsum Wallboard or 5/8" Fire-Shield MR Board nailed both sides 2 x 4 studs, 24" o.c.	38	NGC 2404
			FM	W16B–1hr.			
			GA	WP 3510			
SINGLE LAYER (resilient)							
4	1 hr.		UL	Based on U305	5/8" Fire-Shield Gypsum Wallboard, screw applied to Gold Bond Resilient Furring Channel, spaced 24" o.c. one side only on 2 x 4 studs spaced 16" o.c. Other side 5/8" Fire-Shield Gypsum Wallboard or 5/8" Fire-Shield MR Board nailed direct to studs.	43	NGC 2367
			FM	Based on W16A–1 hr.			
			GA	WP 3605			
5	1 hr.		WHI	694-0200	5/8" Fire-Shield G Gypsum Wallboard, screw applied to Gold Bond Resilient Furring Channel spaced 24" o.c. one side only, on 2 x 4 studs spaced 24" o.c. Other side 5/8" Fire-Shield G Gypsum Wallboard screw attached direct to studs. 3" mineral wool (3 pcf) in stud cavity.	50	Based on TL 77-138
			GA	Based on WP 3230			
DOUBLE LAYER							
6	1 hr.		FM	W9–1 hr. (WP-147)	1/2" Fire-Shield G Wallboard or 1/2" Fire-Shield G Durasan laminated to 1/4" gypsum sound deadening wallboard nailed to both sides 2 x 4 studs, spaced 16" o.c.	45	NGC 2321
			GA	WP 3341			
7	2 hr.		FM	W8–2hr. (WP-360)	5/8" Fire-Shield Gypsum Wallboard base layer nail applied to both sides 2 x 4 wood studs, spaced 24" o.c. Face layer 5/8" Fire-Shield Gypsum Wallboard nail applied.	40	Based on NGC 2363
			GA	WP 4135			
8	est. 2 hr.		FM	Based on W8–2 hr. (WP-360)	Two layers 5/8" Fire-Shield Gypsum Wallboard nailed one side to 2 x 4 wood studs, 16" o.c. Two layers other side screw applied to Gold Bond Resilient Furring channels spaced 24" o.c.	50	NGC 2368
			GA	WP 4135			
9	2 hr.		FM	Based on W8–2 hr. (WP-360)	Two layers 5/8" Fire-Shield Wallboard nailed (24" o.c. base layer 8" o.c. face layer) to 2 x 4 wood studs 16" o.c. staggered 8" o.c. Single 6" plate.	51	NGC 2377
			GA	WP 3910			
10	2 hr.		FM	Based on W8–2 hr. (WP-360)	5/8" Fire-Shield Wallboard base layer applied vertically, nailed 24" o.c. Face Layer 5/8" Fire-Shield Wallboard applied horizontally, nailed 8" o.c. Double row of 2 x 4 wood studs 16" o.c. on separate plates, sound rating with 3 1/2" mineral wool or glass fiber in cavity.	58	NGC 3056
			GA	WP 3820			
11	2 hr.		UL	U301	Two layers of 5/8" Fire-Shield Gypsum Wallboard nail applied to 2 x 4 wood studs spaced 16" o.c. Boards may be applied horizontally or vertically with all joints staggered.	40	NGC 2363
			GA	Based on WP 4135			

GOLD BOND GYPSUM PARTITION AND CEILING SYSTEMS

National Gypsum Company produces a variety of products for construction in its Gold Bond Building Products. These products are mostly provided for development of interior wall and ceiling systems.

The data shown here is taken from one of their recent catalogs and shows some variations of a basic form of construction for interior partitions and for typical floor/ceiling assemblies. This is a small sample of data available from the manufacturer.

STC values are given for both wall and floor systems. IIC values are given for the floor assemblies.

Manufacturer: National Gypsum Company

QUICK SELECTOR FOR SOUND AND FIRE RATED ASSEMBLIES

Floor/Ceilings – Wood Framing (wood joists with rough and finished floor)

No.	Fire Rating		Ref.	Design No.	Description	STC	Test No.	IIC	
								No Carpet	Carpet & Pad
SINGLE LAYER									
1	1 hr.		UL	L522	1/2" Fire-Shield G Gypsum Wallboard nail attached to 2 x 10 wood joists spaced 16" o.c. UL design L522 permits option of floor topping over plywood.	37	NGC 4042 NGC 5032A NGC 5033	32	66
			FM	FC6A–1 hr.					
			GA	FC 5410					
	1 hr.		UL	L501	5/8" Fire-Shield Gypsum Wallboard or 5/8" F.S. Soffit Board nail attached to 2 x 10 wood joists spaced 16" o.c. UL design L501 permits option of Floor Topping Mixture over plywood.	37	Based on NGC 4024	32	66
			FM	FC6B–1 hr.					
			GA	FC 5420					
RESILIENT ATTACHMENT									
2	1 hr.		UL	L515	1/2" Fire-Shield G Gypsum Wallboard screw attached to Resilient Furring Channels spaced 24" o.c. on 2 x 10 wood joists 16" o.c. Wallboard secured to channels with 1" self-drilling screws 12" o.c. Option in UL L515 allows Drywall Suspension System to be hung from joists. No insulation in plenum.	45	NGC 4010 NGC 4107 NGC 5161 NGC 5165	39	63
			FM	FC2B–1 hr.					
			FM	FC181–1 hr.	With 3 1/2" glass fiber.	est. 50			
3	1 hr.		FM	FC193–1 hr.	1/2" Fire-Shield G Gypsum Wallboard attached to Resilient Furring Channels spaced 24" o.c. with screws spaced 12" Elastizell concrete floor 1 1/2" thick, 3 1/2" mineral wool or glass fiber insulation 2 x 10 wood joists 16" o.c.	58	OC-2MT		
			GA	FC 5010					
					Without insulation.	est. 50			

NOTES FOR USE OF QUICK SELECTOR

The construction systems shown here are representative of the many Gold Bond Drywall partitions and ceilings that are performance-verified by laboratory tests. For a given Fire Resistance Rating or Sound Isolation value, simply scan the appropriate columns. Design references prefixed by "Based on..." are extrapolations from test data on similar assemblies. In all cases, the variation does not diminish its fire resistive qualities below its assigned rating.

In the drawings, in metal-stud partitions where insulation is shown in half of the partition cavity, the insulation is required for sound ratings only. Where shown across full cavity, insulation is required for fire rating.

In the following Quick Selector, Factory Mutual Design Numbers are the Construction Designations shown in the FM "Specification Tested Products Guide." Numbers shown in parentheses are FM Design Numbers shown in FM test reports and on the Factory Mutual labels imprinted on Gold Bond Fire-Shield Wallboards.

In the following listings, 5/8" Fire-Shield G Gypsum Wallboard may be substituted for 5/8" Fire-Shield in all designs listed for 5/8" Fire-Shield. 5/8" Fire-Shield G must be used in designs listed for 5/8" Fire-Shield G.

Descriptions in the Quick Selector tables are resumes. For copies of tests and/or for detailed information, consult your Gold Bond representative or local district sales office.

KEY TO ABBREVIATIONS:

- **U.L.** – Underwriters Laboratories, Inc.
- **O.S.U.** – Building Research Laboratories. The Ohio State University
- **F.M.** – Factory Mutual Research Corporation
- **G.A.** – Gypsum Association
- **O.C.** – Owens-Corning Fiberglas Corp.
  (Tests by Geiger & Hamme)
- **BBN** – Bolt Beranek & Newman
- **TL** – Indicates tests for Gold Bond Building Products, A National Gypsum Division by Riverbank Acoustical Laboratories
- **NGC** – Gold Bond Building Products, A National Gypsum Division
- **WHI** – Warnock-Hersey International, Inc.
- **U. of Cal.** – University of California
- **PFS** – PFS Corporation

Manufacturer: National Gypsum Company

Sound-SHIELD
Sound Control Batts

Basic Use: Sound-SHIELD fiber glass sound control batts are designed for use in press-fit installations, without stapling or fastening, between wood or steel studs in walls and in floor/ceiling system applications. The unfaced fiber glass batts are made to fit standard spacing and thickness of steel stud construction in commercial and institutional buildings. They are designed to stay in place and provide maximum sound control effectiveness by completely filling the cavity wall.

Composition and Materials: These batts are produced from lightweight, sound-absorbent insulation made of long resilient glass fibers, bonded with a thermosetting resin.

Sizes: Sound-SHIELD is designed to a thickness of 2³/4" (70mm), 4" (102mm) and 6³/4" (171mm) in order to completely fill the steel cavity (for 2¹/2", 3⁵/8" and 6" steel studs).

Limitations: Material should not be exposed to weather during shipping and storage. Once Sound-SHIELD has been delivered to the job site, it should be protected with a weatherproof cover or tarpaulin, or stored indoors.

Fire Ratings: Sound-SHIELD meets the non-combustible criteria of ASTM E 136 and has a low flame spread/smoke developed rating of 25/50 or less per ASTM E 84. A wood or steel stud wall having one layer of ⁵/8" thick Type X gypsum board on each side has a 1 hour rating per ASTM E 119. With ¹/2" thick Type X gypsum board, the rating is 45 minutes. Since fiber glass is a non-combustible material, Sound-SHIELD when properly installed in the cavities between the studs, does not reduce the fire rating of the construction.

Ceiling assembly ratings vary by construction. Consult a gypsum board or ceiling system supplier for the hourly fire rating of the assembly.

2¹/2" Steel Studs

2¹/2" steel studs: single layer ¹/2" Type X gypsum board each side; 1 thickness 2³/4" (70mm) fiber glass Sound-SHIELD sound control batts

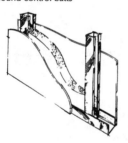

STC 45

2¹/2" steel studs: single layer ⁵/8" Type X gypsum board each side; 1 thickness 2³/4" (70mm) fiber glass Sound-SHIELD sound control batts

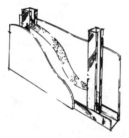

STC 47

2¹/2" steel studs: double layer ¹/2" Type X gypsum board one side, single layer other side; 1 thickness 2³/4" (70mm) fiber glass Sound-SHIELD sound control batts

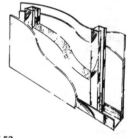

STC 52

2¹/2" steel studs: double layer ⁵/8" Type X gypsum board 1 side, single layer other side; 1 thickness 2³/4" (70mm) fiber glass Sound-SHIELD sound control batts

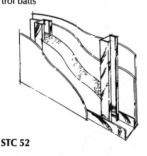

STC 52

2¹/2" steel studs: double layer ¹/2" Type X gypsum board each side; 1 thickness 2³/4" (70mm) fiber glass Sound-SHIELD sound control batts

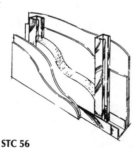

STC 56

2¹/2" steel studs: double layer ⁵/8" Type X gypsum board each side; 1 thickness 2³/4" (70mm) fiber glass Sound-SHIELD sound control batts

STC 57

Manufacturer: Schuller International, Inc., Building Insulation Division

3⅝" Steel Studs

3⅝" steel studs: single layer ½" Type X gypsum board each side; 1 thickness 4" (102mm) fiber glass Sound-SHIELD sound control batts

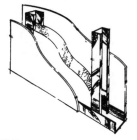

STC 49

3⅝" steel studs: single layer ⅝" Type X gypsum board each side; 1 thickness 4" (102mm) fiber glass Sound-SHIELD sound control batts

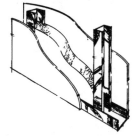

STC 50

3⅝" steel studs: double layer ½" Type X gypsum board 1 side, single layer other side; 1 thickness 4" (102mm) fiber glass Sound-SHIELD sound control batts

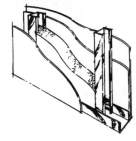

STC 53

3⅝" steel studs: double layer ⅝" Type X gypsum board 1 side, single layer other side; 1 thickness 4" (102mm) fiber glass Sound-SHIELD sound control batts

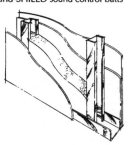

STC 55

3⅝" steel studs: double layer ½" Type X gypsum board each side; 1 thickness 4" (102mm) fiber glass Sound-SHIELD sound control batts

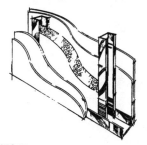

STC 56

3⅝" steel studs: double layer ⅝" Type X gypsum board each side; 1 thickness 4" (102mm) fiber glass Sound-SHIELD sound control batts

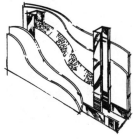

STC 59

6" Steel Studs

6" steel studs: single layer ⅝" Type X gypsum board each side; 1 thickness 6¾" (171mm) fiber glass Sound-SHIELD sound control batts

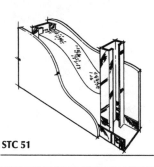

STC 51

6" steel studs, resilient channels: single layer ⅝" Type X gypsum board each side; 1 thickness 6¾" (171mm) fiber glass Sound-SHIELD sound control batts

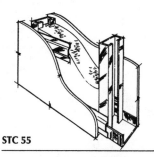

STC 55

6" steel studs, resilient channels: double layer ⅝" Type X gypsum board 1 side, single layer other side; 1 thickness 6¾" (171mm) fiber glass Sound-SHIELD sound control batts

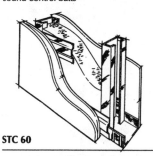

STC 60

Manufacturer: Schuller International, Inc., Building Insulation Division

STUDY AIDS

This section provides the reader with some means to measure his or her comprehension and skill development with regard to the book presentations. When the study of a chapter is completed, the reader should use the materials in this section to find out what has been accomplished. The Index and Glossary can be used to find definitions of the words and terms. Answers to the general questions are given at the end of this section.

WORDS AND TERMS

For each chapter indicated, review the meaning and significance of the following words and terms.

Chapter 1

Room acoustics
Sound privacy
Noise
Noise control
Hearing (listening) task
Ambient (background) noise

Masking sound
Suppression of noise source
Noise transmission
Audibility
Echo
Focusing
Vibration
Murphy's laws

Chapter 2

Sound wave
Sound pressure
Frequency
Hertz
Speed of sound travel
Wavelength
Decibel
Loudness
Apparent loudness: frequency plus loudness
Range of hearing: frequency and level
Pitch
Timbre
Tone
Pure tone
Overtone
Harmonic
Complex sound
Oscillogram
Direct sound path
Reflected sound path
Absorption
Sound reinforcement
Reverberation
Diffraction
Resonance
Airborne sound
Structure-borne sound

Chapter 3

Hearing
Auditory spectrum
Sound path
Sound distribution
Building occupancy

Chapter 4

Sabin
Sound absorption coefficient
Noise reduction coefficient (NCR)
Reverberation time
Dead/live sound (space)

Chapter 5

Noise source
Attenuation of sound transmission
Sound transmission class (STC)

Chapter 6

Noise paths: flanking, leak, channeled
Isolation of source
Insulation of listeners

Chapter 7

Impact noise
Impact insulation class (IIC)

GENERAL QUESTIONS

Chapter 1

1. What are the three general areas of concern for sound control in buildings?

2. Describe the common types of situations in buildings that create sound control problems.

3. What situation must exist for noise to be a "problem"?

4. What are the three basic ways to reduce the effect of a noise problem?

5. What modern trends contribute to make sound privacy in buildings an increasing problem?

6. What listener response factors contribute to making sound control optimization goals difficult to define in terms of specific data?

Chapter 2

1. What are the significant differences between sound travel through the air and through solids?

2. How is loudness of sound quantified (a) in relative descriptive terms (apparent loudness); (b) in numerical units?

3. Why is measurement of sound levels in decibels of more direct use for sound control design?

4. What is the significance of a decibel level of zero?

5. Why is the apparent loudness of sounds not related to decibel level alone?

6. For a listener, what adds to the effect of direct sound travel from sound source to listener in an enclosed space?

Chapter 3

1. What principal factors make it difficult to develop optimal hearing conditions for a group of listeners?

2. What types of intruding noise tend to be most disturbing for listeners?

3. Of what purpose for design for sound control is the identification of occupancy as defined by building codes?

Chapter 4

1. Since the absorption of sound by a surface varies with changes in frequency (Hz), what is the significance of the single-value coefficient called the NRC?

2. What is good and bad about reverberation?

3. If noise is basically unwanted sound, how can a background noise level serve a useful purpose?

4. What physical properties affect the behavior of a sound-reflecting surface?

Chapter 5

1. Of all methods available, what is the first choice for control of the effect of a noise source?

2. What makes it difficult for building designers to control sound in buildings planned for speculative occupancy (undetermined future tenants)?

3. Besides directly or by transmission through barriers, how does noise travel from a source to listeners?

4. What are some major reasons why structure-borne noise is especially difficult to control?

5. How is reverberation related to background noise?

6. What is the difference between sound insulation and sound isolation?

7. How can architectural planning affect sound control?

8. Once building planning and development of the basic construction have been finalized, what special additional measures may be used to enhance the building for noise control?

Chapter 6

1. What are the three basic techniques for controlling airborne noise?

2. Since the transmission behavior of sound barriers varies for different frequencies, how can a single transmission value (STC) be used effectively for design?

Chapter 7

1. What are the three elements that constitute a structure-borne noise problem?

2. What must be done to a structure to reduce its ability to transmit sound?

3. What is the most effective means for reduction of transmission of impact noise?

ANSWERS TO THE GENERAL QUESTIONS

Chapter 1

1. Room acoustics, sound privacy, and noise control.

2. Noisy rooms next to quiet ones; adjacent spaces bothering each other; noise from building equipment; intrusive noises from outside the building.

3. It must disturb someone with a sound privacy or hearing task goal.

4. Suppress the source; attenuate the transmission; isolate the listeners.

5. More noise sources; increasingly lighter construction; tighter packing of buildings and people; increased expectations of building users for comfort.

6. Individuals vary in terms of hearing ability, sound-conditioning experience, expectations for sound privacy, and ability to concentrate for listening tasks.

Chapter 2

1. Travel through solids is much faster and much more efficient (less loss of sound energy in transit).

2. (a) Barely audible, too loud, too too loud; (b) in decibels.

3. The unit base is the threshold of hearing for human ears; it is a relative measurement based on a regular increment of apparent loudness increase for human beings. This makes it more directly related to real human experiences rather than some abstract scientific measurement.

4. It is a sound level established as the threshold (lower limit) of hearing for most human listeners. Sounds above this level can be heard; below it they are mostly indistinguishable as sound.

5. Human hearing ability varies with frequency; some sound frequencies are easily heard, some are difficult to hear, some cannot be discerned as sound.

6. Secondary sounds caused by reflections from the various surfaces in the room.

Chapter 3

1. Individuals vary in hearing ability and in conditioning from experience; listeners are in different positions and locations in a room with respect to sources and reflecting surfaces.

2. Those that are of a nature related to the listener's hearing task; similar in frequency or type. Also those with high levels of intensity in the frequencies to which the ear is most sensitive.

3. Building code occupancy classifications sometimes define listener situations or hearing tasks (office, school, housing, etc.).

Chapter 4

1. It identifies behavior in the general range of sound frequencies of greatest sensitivity for the human ear.

2. It can add to the quality of the sound or even to audibility in terms of reinforcement from reflected sounds. It can also drown out the direct sounds if the reflections endure too long, reducing audibility or causing ringing, garbling, or roaring effects.

3. It can serve to increase sound privacy or reduce the annoying effects of incoming noises.

4. Distance from source and listeners; size of reflecting surface; surface texture (absorption, diffraction, etc.); shape of surface (flat, convex, etc.); angle of surface with respect to direct sound and location of listeners; structural character (soft, rigid, etc.).

Chapter 5

1. Usually, the suppression or isolation of the noise source.

2. Exact requirements of future tenants is speculative; manipulation of interior construction is in hands of other, undetermined, future designers.

3. By reflections, through channels, by flanking, by leaks in barriers, as structure-borne.

4. The building structure is harder to modify than are nonstructural elements of the construction. Most structures have considerable continuity (continous materials and elements or hard connections). The

sound travel is extremely efficient, making loss with distance of separation very low. Many of the worst noise sources are typically coupled to the structure for efficient sound transmission.

5. Both are essentially enduring sound. Reverberation can magnify or amplify background noise. If background noise from direct sources is high, reverberation may be less distinguishable.

6. Isolation is the basic removal of either the source or the listener from the sound transmission. An insulated enclosure is one means of achieving isolation.

7. Avoid placing sensitive listeners near noise sources; use natural buffers for separation (corridors, storage rooms, etc.); use room shape, size, and proportions of dimensions to best advantage for sound control of individual spaces.

8. Modify the basic construction (seal leaks, use alternative surfacing, etc.); increase insulative properties of barriers with different materials or details; use isolation devices or details in the sound transmission paths; use added background noise.

Chapter 6

1. See Question 1, Chapter 4: suppress the source if possible—first choice; isolate the listener—by distance, by an insulative enclosure, and so on; generally modify the transmission pathways to lose as much of the source noise energy along the way as possible.

2. The STC value is based on an evaluation of behavior in the narrow range of frequencies most critical for the human ear. It is established by shifting of the barrier response over the range of tested frequencies to as close a fit as possible to a standard noise reduction curve, implying a larger response evaluation than the single STC value indicates.

Chapter 7

1. A noise source coupled to the structure; a continuous structure between the source and an affected listener; and a listener positioned so that the structure-borne vibrations may be both "felt" as vibration and heard as airborne sound.

2. Isolate it from either the noise source or affected listeners. Cause an interruption in its continuity (soft joint) along the transmission path.

3. Surface absorption (cushioning).

INDEX